YOU'RE NOT BROKE, YOU'RE BROKEN

HOW TO MOVE PAST YOUR FINANCIAL FAILURES

JAY GAUDET

Published by Freiling Agency, LLC.

P.O. Box 1264
Warrenton, VA 20188

www.FreilingAgency.com

PB ISBN: 978-1-963701-42-5
E-book ISBN: 978-1-963701-43-2

TABLE OF CONTENTS

Foreword by Mink Gaudet...v
Preface ix
Acknowledgements...xiii
Introduction..xvii

1   Amy From Ocwen 1
2   YOLO..11
3   Scared Money Don't Make Money 23
4   High Jump...33
5   Top Hats..41
6   The Shoebox 49
7   Got Milk..59
8   School Shoes 65
9   Free Throws 73
10   Educated Fool..83
11   La Margie...91
12   The House Room..97
13   Revelation Horse..109
14   Treat Yourself, Don't Cheat Yourself...................115
15   Twenty...125
16   The Fourth Generation 133

FOREWORD

By Mink Gaudet

—◦◦◦—

Brokenness is a powerful state—one that can drag us into the depths of grief or trap us in cycles of disassociation that feed the ego but never mend the wounds.

Healing, on the other hand, is freedom. Yet, it's not easy. It's raw, messy, and profoundly lonely—a journey into the darkest parts of yourself. But it's a journey worth taking. Because even though the process is ongoing, it leads to the most radiant, truest version of yourself.

The version God designed you to be—a reflection of the shadows you've faced but also an embodiment of true, divine beauty.

And beauty is the strength to rise from brokenness, to carry your scars with grace, and to live as a testament to the light that heals.

This book, *You're Not Broke, You're Broken*, is a reflection of Jay's own journey through brokenness to healing. It's an honest, vulnerable, and inspiring account of what it takes to break free from the cycles that hold us back and step into the fullness of who we are meant to be.

I am so proud of Jay for sharing this part of himself with the world. His insights, lessons, and unwavering faith are sure to inspire and empower everyone who reads these pages.

With love and admiration,

Your Loving Wife - Mink Gaudet

MLYB

PREFACE

—⟨∞⟩—

W ell, first off, I want to thank you for your support.

I wrote this book because, over the last few years, I've been more confused about this subject matter than I've ever been in my life. As I continued to learn and study money and the psychology behind it, I realized it's one of the most blatantly unsolved mysteries known to man. What amazed me even more was how little protest and advocacy exist around normalizing the education and training of financial literacy.

It's my goal that everyone reading this book not only gains wisdom and insight from the connection of my personal financial stories—stories deeply intertwined with the impact of financial trauma, triggers, and psychology—but also develops positive financial habits. These habits, when nurtured, can serve as the foundation for implementing and executing strategies that build generational wealth.

I pray that this book serves as a bridge between understanding the emotional relationship we have with money and taking actionable steps toward financial independence and empowerment. It's about breaking cycles, rewriting narratives, and creating a legacy that thrives far beyond today.

Thank you for taking this journey with me. Let's change the way we think about money, one step at a time.

ACKNOWLEDGEMENTS

I would like to express my deepest appreciation to those who inspired me to write this book. First, I would like to thank my high school basketball coach, Derrick Jones, for introducing me to the concept of mental toughness. In my hardest days and darkest nights, I always remember the numbers on the time clock, fifty-eight seconds, struggling to finish the sixteen sideline sprints. It was those times that taught me quitting isn't an option, and conditioning is preparation for when you think you're defeated. Secondly, I'd like to thank my mom, my cousin Dairy, and my Aunt Brenda, for being the people in my life who, no matter what, I could depend on. I love you and will be forever grateful for the investments you all made in my life. I'd like to thank my publisher for his insight and commitment on this project. Lastly, I want to express my deepest gratitude to my lovely wife. For the last twelve years, you have been my rock, nurturing me, encouraging me, supporting me, and challenging me to be the best version of myself. Creating a space for me to be vulnerable and not just grow, but grow up. Without you there is no me, I love you and I thank you as I dedicate my first book to you.

INTRODUCTION

—❦—

Watching your mother split a hamburger in two to feed you and your baby sister really takes a toll on an adolescent kid. Looking up at her while she struggles to be a pillar of strength, regardless of her efforts, you see the moments of weakness. That type of experience with deprivation not only changes you, it breaks you. It develops a mindset in your subconscious that automatically adopts a false association with money, equating it to survival.

The use of money is a trained behavior. No matter if you use it in the most advanced way, meaning you have been able to generate a substantial degree of wealth, or if you misuse it and you have repeatedly ended up in the same money cycle; you were trained either consciously or subconsciously on how you use your funds.

That encounter was not my first encounter with the harsh reality of my family's financial environment. Up until I was twelve years old, I grew up in the house with both parents and my little sister. Like many married couples that are in financially strained situations, my parents argued about money all the time. My dad was an electrician by trade, he made a decent income but had limited job security. Between layoffs, firings, and most times a flawed position on financial decision making, the flow of cash was extremely inconsistent in the Gaudet home. My mom was an entrepreneur and eventually became a real estate broker. I always knew when my mom would sell a house or come into a lump sum of money. She would do nice things for us like take us out to eat, buy us new clothes, or do something around the house.

My parents' posture on how to manage finances was, when money came in, find something to do with the money because you do not know when you will get it again. If she closed on a house, this was the opportunity to make a major repair or renovation, if there was an insurance settlement, this was an opportunity to purchase or consume things that their normal day-to-day income would not support.

I was born on February 6, 1988, in Beaumont, Texas, to Harold Gaudet and Yvette Daniels. My mother, an educated woman, with a college degree, was the strictly business type from New Orleans, Louisiana. My mother had five sisters. My grandfather was an active marine and my grandmother was a seamstress. My mom grew up with little money, but because my grandmother was skilled with a needle, she and my aunts always looked the part, custom dresses, they always showed out, regardless of their financial situation.

My dad was from a country town called Edgard, Louisiana, population less than 1,800 people where the town joke was: it's the town with no traffic lights. My dad had eleven brothers and sisters. My dad wasn't the planning type, didn't believe in making future financial decisions unless it was counting his money before he got it. He was and still is, the live-in-the-now type of guy. My parents got married the year before I was born, they were both hustlers, knew exactly how to make a dollar, but we found out through many life experiences that making money is the easy part. The challenge is understanding how you get off the hamster wheel of exchanging time for money and experiencing minimal reward for your labors. The million dollar question: is your money serving you, or are you serving your money?

I grew up on the Westbank of New Orleans, Louisiana. Where I come from, the topic of wealth and money was a taboo subject matter. In most cases, if money was being discussed, the discussion was not having enough of it. Black people were expected to struggle and for the rare few that didn't, it was as if they were some anomaly. Positive financial affirmation was not a thing growing up in a black household in the '90s. It was the norm to hear your parents say things like, "Do you think money grows on trees?" or "When we go in this store, don't ask me for nothing." We didn't see these things as having a negative effect on our future relationship with money, this was just the way things were. It was the norm in a black household if you wanted more and you didn't have the money to buy, you became resourceful. You wanted nice clothes, you learned how to sew. You wanted a car, and wanted to keep it, you learned how to work under the hood. You wanted to eat, at the very least, you learned how to cook. I learned to sew at the age of ten. I would sew the holes in my socks to avoid asking my mom to buy me new pairs. Of course my mom would have found a way to buy me more socks if I would have told her that mine had holes in them, but that was the mindset of a young black boy in a home where he's aware of his financially strained environment. You just make do and do your best to not need as much.

Not having everything you want in life rarely comes from the lack of ability. God gave every single human being on this earth a unique gift that could be traded as the most precious commodity. In His perfect will, money would be obsolete because every individual's gift is so unique, so specific, that it could be traded as a good or service. It's unfortunate that many die with that gift or will live a life where that gift never reaches its full potential.

It's rare that children actually listen to their parents and put into action the wisdom that they tirelessly try to deliver. But it's very common for children to adopt the behaviors of their parents, good, bad, and/or ugly. Ask yourself, what is the real purpose of money? Some say to survive, some would say to live, some would say to buy nice things, but most of us miss the mark. You with a dollar bill is no different than a carpenter with a hammer or Steph Curry with a basketball. Money is merely a tool designed for you to use to give you daily freedom to live out your God-given talent purposefully through God's will.

Through centuries of oppression, our ancestors' daily mission was to survive, to do what was required to make it to the next day. We aren't so removed from that reality today. Still today, a thirty-five-year-old can have a conversation with an elderly family member that can still remember a close relative that was in slavery. So, what happens to a generation of people who were never money-trained? What happens when your sole money foundation is built from survival, depravity, and consumerism? The result is you are omitted from all wealth-building principles. Your mind won't allow you to conceive thoughts of abundance, production, or giving because your ability to earn will only matter to afford you the ability to maintain your current situation. To break this mentality you have to work extremely hard to break your subconscious mind because this will shape the way you earn, spend, and invest money.

Because of my pursuit of money, I sold drugs, went to college, started businesses, made a bunch of money, and lost it all, because I was still money stupid with horrible money behaviors. Money decisions have a lifetime of effects. The great thing is smart money decisions can have a lifetime of positive effects and, to the contrary, poor money decisions could have a lifetime of negative effects. Sometimes the decisions that you make may not have anything to do with money. It could be the person you decide to be in a relationship with, the place you decide to live, or how you decide to start a family.

I was prompted to write this book because as I reflect on my childhood, my teenage years, and my twenties, I ask myself, how did I get here? How did I become so entrenched in the financial industry when no part of my environment supported this trajectory?

As black kids, we are exposed to America's norm. I grew up watching shows like *The Fresh Prince*, *Martin*,

The Cosby Show, and *New York Undercover*. These were all examples of what black excellence looked like to the adolescent youth. Our parents taught us about going the safe route, becoming a doctor, a lawyer, or a police officer. Career pathways in black households were presented to depict security first, not purpose or passion. The theme was you could enter a career field if it pays well and you would have job security, even if you don't like what you do.

In my career, I sold drugs, got two college degrees, started and sold companies, and worked for the government and private sector. I have found one commonality in every venture that I have pursued in my adult life. No matter what business you are in, what career field, or how much your salary is, you are only successful and able to afford the lifestyle that you desire if you master the art of money management.

My exposure to the financial industry came about from my career in real estate. The best deals that got through were those that had the best financial package, and to create those deals you had to understand how money moved. You've heard the saying, money makes the world go round, a very true statement, so why aren't we represented in an environment built to create generational wealth.

Up until the age of fifteen, I still did not have my own relationship with money. I earned money over the years here and there, doing odd jobs and different hustles, but never to the extent of really earning my own money and managing the money I earned.

Approaching my freshman year in highschool, my parents recently divorced. We were experiencing one of the hardest financial seasons that I had witnessed in my life. My mom came to my room and told me that she couldn't afford to buy us new uniforms and shoes for school and we would have to wear what we had from last year. This was where survival mode kicked in. Every money experience that I witnessed up until that point was cultivated through survival and I was about to repeat that cycle. At that time, I did the only thing that I knew to do. I called my older brother to connect me with a dealer and I took my only $50 and bought my first package of marijana.

1

AMY FROM OCWEN

I want you to try something. Go back in time, think about your adolescent self and reminisce on the memories you have specifically about money. Think about the first time you had your own money to spend, the first conversation you heard your parents have about money, or the first time you wanted money for your own.

Now think about your present self. Regardless if what you uncovered on your trip down memory lane was good or bad, is it safe to say that you can identify some similarities with the money behaviors that you display in your adulthood? Financial behaviors are deeply ingrained in the experiences that we have encountered over our lifespan, most beginning with our childhood, often learned from our immediate environment from what we observed and lived through. Amongst the four primary financial archetypes—the conservative saver, the impulsive spender, the prudent avoider, and the overspender. Who wouldn't want to have the behaviors of financial alchemy which displays the ability to use money with such mastery that it multiplies for generations? It's the latter who comprehends the potency of money as a tool for wealth creation. The exemplars, such as Buffet, Bezos, and Musk, didn't merely rely on access or resources, they mastered the art of making money work for them, cultivated through years of disciplined financial stewardship.

I took that same journey down memory lane, and the very first memory that came to recollection was Amy. To my imagination, Amy was a white female, with dark brown hair and cold brown eyes. Her voice was very crisp and clear and she was very articulate. I never physically met Amy, but she would call every day. When I was in the fifth grade, school would let out at 3:00 p.m., and by time I walked home, got inside, used the bathroom, and turned on the TV, I could expect the phone to ring and see the bright light on the caller ID that read Amy from Ocwen Federal Bank. The reality that I faced at a later part in my life was that the calls from Amy weren't for pleasantries. Although her disposition to the comprehension of a ten year old was that she was a friend of the family, she wasn't, that explained the one time that Amy called, and my mom was home and I happily answered the phone and brought it to her, she immediately scolded me for it. Amy was actually seeking communication with my mom to foreclose on our home. Recalling persistent correspondences from Amy at the mortgage institution reflects the reality faced by my parents. While both possessed an entrepreneurial drive, a lack of financial discipline impeded long-term financial stability, leading to the looming threat of foreclosure. This wasn't solely due to inconsistent work patterns but rooted in an overall deficiency of financial preparedness.

My family returned to New Orleans in '93 after relocating from Columbus, Ohio. This move marked a significant shift. Eager for a home to replicate the life we departed from, my parents hastily planned without aligning their aspirations with their financial realities. My father's sporadic work history made his income unstable for such a significant commitment. The prudent choice would have been to continue residing with my grandmother until a stable financial foundation supported the purchase of a home for a family of four, a decision demanding patience and a willingness to endure temporary discomfort, a choice they were reluctant to embrace.

Parents often assert they act in the best interests of their children, yet decisions made on their behalf occasionally disregard their actual necessities. Our close living quarters in my grandmother's house were a testament to this. Nevertheless, amidst the space constraints, I cherished the intimacy shared with my family.

Misconceptions about debt often lead to financial mismanagement. The misunderstanding of debt as a surrogate for cash has kept many individuals living beyond their means, impeding their path to financial independence. Even my mother's guidance on credit card usage, though well-intentioned, contradicted the financial behaviors witnessed at home, emphasizing the overwhelming influence of modeled behavior over verbal guidance, we adopt what we see, not what we are told.

Deeply entrenched financial habits are often transmitted across generations. When one generation fails to address money management issues, these patterns persist, shaping the financial destinies of subsequent generations. It's not solely about income. It's about the deliberate management of finances that defines financial health, often showcased by how individuals handle windfalls—illuminating their inherent financial dispositions.

The persisting calls from Amy at the mortgage institution serve as a consequence of my parents' lack of fiscal readiness. Financial responsibility isn't just about income. It pivots on prudent expenditure, sustainable earnings, purposeful savings, and astute investments for the future.

However, the inclination for desires to overshadow preparedness often leads to permanent decisions rooted in transient circumstances. My father's persuasiveness and their mortgage qualifications led us to our new home, a decision seemingly plausible on the surface but predicated more on optimism than financial prudence.

Ultimately, the journey toward financial wisdom and life choices bears resemblance to the profound quest for a life partner. Both necessitate a nuanced understanding of desires and preparedness, weaving together the fabric of our futures. Just as selecting a life partner goes beyond fleeting emotions, financial acumen transcends momentary desires. It's a continual amalgamation of aspirations, realities, and a willingness to heed the lessons etched into our experiences. Navigating these terrains, whether in relationships or finances, demands a harmonious balance between aspirations and readiness, guiding us toward choices founded on wisdom, foresight, and the assimilation of invaluable lessons learned.

Our journeys in understanding financial literacy often stem from the lessons taught and observed during childhood. My father's occasional endeavors as an independent

contractor and my mother's resilient efforts as an entrepreneur both emphasized the unpredictability of income,
inadvertently shaping my outlook on financial stability.

Returning to the Big Easy at the cusp of adolescence
brought an abrupt shift in perspective. The vibrant city
pulsated with cultural richness, but beneath the surface
lay the stark economic disparities. Living in the heart of
a city with contrasting pockets of affluence and struggle
instilled a deeper appreciation for fiscal prudence and
social responsibility.

My teenage years were a blend of discovery and financial awakening. Observing my parents' juggle between
aspirations and financial limitations highlighted the value
of sound fiscal planning, but still lacked the necessary
training. The consistent witness of the practice of "robbing
Peter to pay Paul" instilled a survivalist ethos within me.
The importance of distinguishing between wants, needs,
and bare necessities became a recurring theme in our
household discussions, shaping my perception of long-
term financial health.

Financial therapy was a groundbreaking discovery for
me. Luckily for me, my wife holds a degree in psychology
and is a Certified Financial Therapist. One of the most
frustrating nuances is to repeat the same negative habit,
being fully conscious that you are doing something that
will deliver negative future results, but you do it anyway.
This was me when it came to my finances. I got to a point
in my life where I had to deeply self reflect to identify
where the habit started.

During early adulthood, I painfully overspent, did not save, and overleveraged. I had extreme earning capability, but as money came in, it went out. Identifying that there was a problem, I went back to think about those moments during my childhood. I was quickly able to identify key moments pertaining to money events that were embedded in my subconscious that were the planted seeds for my future money tree.

I used to think checks were magic money. In my eyes, as long as my mom had checks, we had money. I actually think my old man had the same theory. It was a specific event when my mom, my dad, my sister, and I took a trip to the local grocery store. This wasn't a normal event for all four of us to be in the grocery store together, another reason why this event stood out to me. My mom was very focused, she knew what we came to the store to get and she didn't deviate from that. Of course she was the one that knew how much money we had. My dad moved through the aisles, playing with my sister and me, not really paying much attention to the items my mom picked up. When we got to the register, I asked my mom if I could have one of the toy model collector cars. She told me no. I asked her why, remembering that the last few times we went into a store, I saw her pull out a booklet, write something on it, and hand it to the cashier. I remember hearing her and my dad refer to the booklet as a checkbook. When she told me that I couldn't have the toy, my response was, "Why not, Mom? All you have to do is write a check." Not wanting to tell me that we didn't have any money, her response to me was, "Son, we don't have any more checks." I walked over to my dad, sad about my mom's response. He asked me what was wrong, and I said, "Mama said we don't have any more checks, so I can't get the toy." He replied, obviously not aware of our financial situation either, "Oh no, we don't run out of no checks."

When you display habits of financial mismanagement, this is one of the easiest habits to fall into and one of the hardest to break. Because some financial institutions have a lag when processing checks, it can sometimes allow the consumer one to two business days to come up with the funds and make the deposit to cover the transaction they did days prior. This was one of my first money memories, and one of the first financial habits I had to identify and break.

Most of us continue in financial uncertainty because we have not identified that we have negative financial behaviors that stem from past financial trauma. Financial trauma refers to the profound and often lasting emotional, psychological, or behavioral impacts resulting from negative financial experiences. This can stem from various situations such as bankruptcy, significant debt, foreclosure, job loss, or any financial event that creates overwhelming stress, anxiety, or sense of powerlessness.

Going in the store asking for additional items in a financially strained household is a no-no. In many cases, it's safe to say that the parent would love to get their kid a piece of candy, or the toy they like, but they went into the store with a finite budget and any unexpected extras would deplete their budget, or worse, force them to resonate with the reality that they're in financial hardship. Deep down they are frustrated and somewhat embarrassed that they can't give any extra, but their response derives from a trauma response of lack, loss, or some sort of financial disparity. Those quotes that we have heard so many adults say, "Does it look like I'm made of money? Do you think money grows on trees?" These money scripts accompanied by other forms of negative financial behaviors unchecked, result in a pass down of negative relationships with money from generation to generation.

2

YOLO

—◦◦◦—

In South Louisiana, long before climate change and
global warming was really a thing, it was natural to have
real hurricane scares and nothing happened. In 1998, I
remember being in the fifth grade and we had a mandatory
evacuation due to Hurricane George. As kids, a hurricane
scare meant a mini-vacation. I could never understand why
my parents took it so hard though. They were not happy
at all! I later discovered through adulting and having to
support my own family through crisis, that to evacuate for
a hurricane cost money, and in a financially unprepared
household, unplanned circumstances was always a hefty
burden. You have to ask yourself, in life's uncertainty, how
ready are you to withstand a financial blow. Covid-19 was
a great example of why being financially trained is a bare
necessity. We have accelerated far beyond the era of "fake
it till you make it," or "just figuring it out." Those are the
avenues that we are accustomed to taking because preparation in any form takes real work. It takes discipline, grit,
and tenacity. When it comes to our money, remember,
we mentioned this earlier, I can confidently say that you
don't have money issues. You're not broke. You're not
less than the person with the big house and the luxury
cars. You are financially untrained. What is better to be
trained in than the very tool that you use on a daily basis?
Being financially unprepared vacuums the confidence of

any human to pursue the road to progression, whether they consciously desire it or not.

At thirty-five, one of the most profound financial epiphanies that I've had to date, was sitting with the mere facts that my financial future has to include more than what is aligned to self. Now, the norm is most of us don't consider the future cost of caring for an elderly parent, or having to bury a loved one, or even unexpected additions to the family. Someone dies, we are designed to make due, or raise money. Mama or Daddy needs long-term care, we look to what's available within their social security benefits. But how would it look if we planned for those moments twenty years prior?

These things become a reality, and for me it became a function of you have to stay ready because life doesn't give you time to get ready. What I'm describing is a direct revelation of your relationship with money. Among middle-class adults, fewer than 44 percent have emergency savings, while roughly 35 percent of adults with some college education say the same. But why is that? Is it opportunity? Is it education? Yes, those things are a factor, but the foundational issue is that untrained and uncontrolled money behavior causes us to spend more than we earn. As humans, we know right from wrong. We are very aware of the things that are harmful to us. We know that if we are struggling with health issues that we should be dieting and exercising, but somehow we still find a way to justify eating the fried chicken that we love. Or that toxic relationship that we were supposed to leave in the past years ago, but comfort and familiarity continues to bring us back to a place of dysfunction.

We do the same with our money, for many, the dopamine feeling of spending money gives an euphoric high that's only temporary. You knew it was outside your budget, but your emotion associated with the gratification that you received when you completed the transaction, allowed you to justify the act and deal with the financial repercussions later. When it comes to our money, we are undisciplined, point blank, period.

The formula to live below your means is a very simple formula: spend significantly less than you earn, then save, invest, and become an extreme giver.

I found that some of the wealthiest people give astronomical amounts of money to charities, because to give, especially large amounts of money, means you have to have a spirit of abundance. A lack mindset would tell you that you can't give because you don't have enough, but thinking and operating in abundance isn't always about money, we all have something of value to give.

We can never get to the place of saving, investing, and giving if we are living off of 110 percent of our earnings. I'm sure you've heard the saying, "More month than money." Have you ever contemplated how it got that way? Did you one day just wake up and you didn't have enough money to cover your lifestyle? No, many of us are using today's finances to cover expenses from decisions we made twenty years ago. Society has tricked the untrained. Because we weren't trained on the use of the dollar, but we want the same lifestyle as our peers and counterparts, we curate a life that we technically can't afford.

"Money management isn't a sprint, it's a marathon," I once stated during a financial literacy session that I was lecturing, emphasizing the need for steadfastness in nurturing positive financial habits. The room, filled with eager faces, nodded in agreement, comprehending the depth behind the analogy. A few participants shared stories, recounting their intermittent attempts at savings, relative to sporadically picking up a new hobby. During my seminar, one of the attendees, Shay Thompson's story caught my attention. Shay was open about her financial journey, but what she was most open about was her confusion on her decisions to go against what she knew was not positive financial decision making.

Shay, a twenty-seven-year-old female and single mother of two, works for the hospital as an account manager. She makes 45K a year. Both of her children are in elementary school. After taxes, Shay brings home 32K a year, that's $2,666.66 per month in income. The reality is Shay should not spend more than 30 percent of her income on housing, anything above that means her housing is unaffordable. That means that Shay could only afford an apartment or mortgage for $800 per month. Shay disclosed that she did not like the options available to her with her current budget, so she stretched her budget to $1400 per month. Her thought process was she would get a second job, work additional hours to make up the difference, all which are doable scenarios, but not 100 percent secure. Now she's spending more than half of her income on housing. Shay had a car, a Honda that was paid off, but when Capital One sent her a pre-approval in the mail, she immediately began to see herself in that new Mercedes, with the salesman strategically fitting her monthly note into an amount that was digestible for her, she convinced herself that she could afford the car and she would figure out a way to increase her income. Her note is only $465, so she rationalizes with herself, saying, "I deserve to treat myself to something nice." Her insurance is $327. Now she has $474 left for the month and we haven't touched utilities, groceries, cell phone, etc.

So, what happened to Shay? Her desires overshadowed what was right in front of her. Her income was blatantly honest with her and told her exactly what she could afford, but she told herself otherwise. Shay's story mirrors countless individuals grappling with financial crossroads. Identifying her as the archetypal "Overextender" elucidates the profound impact of recognizing and rectifying negative fiscal habits.

There are thousands of Shays in the world, the great thing is your negative money habits can be corrected, if you identify them. In today's fast-paced society, the allure of quick fixes pervades every aspect of life. Instant gratification dominates our choices, hindering the cultivation of sound financial habits. Yet, the irony remains—developing solid fiscal behaviors early on could expedite the fulfillment of our aspirations. We live in a microwavable society where the average human refuses to wait longer than ten minutes for their food to arrive. The irony of where society has cultivated an environment of extreme convenience and the "now" mentality. The reality is, if we developed sound financial behaviors from the beginning, a lot of things that we desire, we wouldn't have to wait as long for.

The effects of financial trauma can have tremendous results when it comes to how one will manage their financial situation. People who have experienced some form of financial trauma, 99.9 percent of the time can find themselves aligning with one of the four financial archetypes. Many people think that you can just start saving money cold turkey. Just wake up one morning and say, "I'm going to start saving today." While you may begin the behavior, and have the best of intentions to do so, what happens when that action is tested by the woes of life, and you haven't developed the financial discipline to continue the positive habit? You do what most people do, treat their saving journey like a side chick and turn it off and on when it's convenient.

Preparation negates fear. Most people fear things they don't know or understand because of the unknown. You're fearful of investing, because you can't solely control the outcome, which ultimately means, you are not fiscally prepared to take financial risk because you have not prepared to endure loss. You're fearful of losing your job, because you have not prepared financially for a crisis. My parents were frustrated when it was time to evacuate for a hurricane, because spending money for a family of four to travel to another state for an unknown amount of days was not in their financial forecast.

You can't prepare for something that you haven't given an identity to. Meaning, if you haven't identified that smoking a pack of cigarettes a day can cause severe health issues, you wont make the necessary preparations to quit smoking. Even further, if your why is not greater than the how, the act of changing a negative habit becomes more like a job than a purpose. You may identify that your smoking habit has put a direct expiration date on your life, but yet you still smoke a pack a day, until you have the revelation that you want to see your granddaughter graduate from kindergarten. Attaching the why gives you a reason to change your habits to live longer.

Your why on becoming financially independent has to be greater than your how. It's something that the mind does when we give ourselves a point of no return. The human will is a remarkable force, and with focus, dedication, and the right tools, an individual can accomplish anything they have set out to accomplish.

Discipline is the foundational habit of becoming money-trained. I cringe when I hear someone say that they are broke. If that is you, today is the last time you speak those words about yourself. Changing habits is no easy task. Most people fail when trying to eliminate a bad habit and develop a good habit, because they are primarily focused on the result. You want to develop a savings habit, so you can have money for a rainy day.

Habit – Saving money. Result – money available when times are tough.

When you tell yourself or someone else that you are broke, you are not just speaking words. You are giving yourself a financial identity. So, instead of when someone asks you a question that warrants an answer about your immediate finances, instead of blurting out that you are broke, try a response that you can still claim your financial confidence. Try saying things like, "My money is tied up right now" or "I did not budget for that." Changing your financial identity becomes the foundation of changing your financial behaviors. If you have always seen yourself as a person who blows money, or a person who is not good with money, you will never encounter positive money results. The way you respond to yourself when it comes to money is just as important as the money itself. Becoming the positive behavior, not the result. Telling yourself, you are a saver, so when you are making money decisions, ask yourself, would a saver do this? You are an investor. You begin to train your mind to check in with yourself to ask, how would an investor look at this situation?

When you become financially prepared, it negates fear of addressing unknown financial territory. Studies show that 25 to 35 percent of individuals stay in unhealthy marriages primarily due to financial concerns or limitations. This is a complex language for being financially untrained and unprepared. The lack of financial preparation can cause you to remain in and/or tolerate failable circumstances with diminished confidence that you would psychologically not tolerate if your financial mental state were stronger.

Before moving into the next chapter, take the money quiz (www.jaygaudet.com) to determine your money archetype. If you are going to take true control of your financial destiny, you first have to know how you view money, what it means to you and what's your real relationship with it.

To know where to go you have to know where you have been. What was your first real encounter with money, who taught it to you? Where and when did you receive your first money disappointment and how did that affect you? Face where you have been financially, look it in the face and develop the positive habits to become the financial powerhouse that you want to be.

3

SCARED MONEY DON'T MAKE MONEY

Your money personality is a deeply rooted biopsycho-social report of the way you view money and the reasons you make the money decisions that you make. Money is very emotional, and depending on how you have been programmed to handle finances, a financial shift can change your mood in an instance. Think about a time where you may have had an increase in finances that was unexpected—a few extra dollars on your paycheck, an unexpected Cash App from a loved one, or a stranger at Starbucks paying for your coffee. These experiences almost instantly changed your emotion for the better. The same thing applies for the worse—your paycheck was less than expected, an unexpected car repair is needed, or a family member needs financial help. These situations can instantly change your emotions for the worse. These emotions equate to the equivalence of the difference between having happiness and having joy.

My parents divorced when I was thirteen, and something developed in me that, at the time, I couldn't identify. It wasn't until later in my adult life that I began to understand this emotion. Being a teenager, silently battling economic hardship, navigating the societal anchors of being a new teen father and the only male figure in the home, I developed a strong sense of avoidance. This emotion came in many forms. It primarily took form in the sense of not having time to give life to feelings. So, when I was hurt, I avoided; when I was broke, I avoided; when I was angry, I avoided; when I was disappointed, I avoided. This emotion programmed me to consistently move on to the next, there was no time to sit with unfulfilled feelings and the most proactive thing to do was to posture up and move on.

This behavior plagued me in my early adult life. As a father and husband, battling with the pursuit to make a life for a family, I became astute in avoiding the obvious issues that were hindering my financial growth. I wasn't afraid of money, I wasn't afraid of risk, but I was terrified of the feeling that "lack" made me feel. I avoided every foundational behavior that was the root cause of my financial situations. When I messed up my credit, I convinced myself that I could just repair it, but ignored the habits that caused me to mess it up in the first place. When I blew large sums of money and was left with nothing to show for it, I avoided the realities of what was the root cause.

When you tell yourself that you are ready to deal with your negative financial behaviors and you create a plan, you step onto the battleground of self-awareness. It's acknowledging the scars, facing the mirror, and deciding to rewrite the script of your money story. As I ventured into this battlefield, I confronted the avoidance that had become my ally in dodging financial struggles.

Understanding the emotional connection to money is profound. It's a symphony of feelings, playing melodies of joy or sorrow depending on the financial score of our lives. The money personality, as deeply rooted as the DNA that defines us, shapes our attitudes, decisions, and reactions to financial shifts. Money, being more than just currency, is a mood shifter. Unexpected financial blessings bring an instant rise in spirits, akin to catching the winning vibe in a song.

Conversely, unexpected financial hits can plunge us into a somber tune. It's the rhythm of financial emotions, swinging between happiness and sadness. Having money, even a little extra, can trigger a surge of happiness. It's the sudden bonus, the unexpected gift, the small win that changes the financial scorecard and instantly lifts the mood. Conversely, financial strain hits us in the gut. A reduced paycheck, unexpected expenses, or the burden of supporting a family member can instantly cast a shadow on our emotions. The sadness of lacking funds is a powerful chord that plays in the background of our lives.

In the intricate dance of human experience, the brain's functions extend beyond cognitive processes, delving into realms as diverse as emotional regulation and financial decision-making. This exploration seeks to unravel the complex interplay between the brain's fight-or-flight response and how humans instinctively avoid negative financial behaviors. As we delve into this connection, we will uncover the physiological and psychological mechanisms that guide individuals in navigating the financial terrain while drawing parallels with the evolutionary survival instincts ingrained in the human brain.

The fight-or-flight response, deeply rooted in our evolutionary history, is a primal reaction to perceived threats. When faced with danger, the brain triggers a cascade of physiological changes aimed at enhancing our ability to confront or escape the threat. This response involves the release of stress hormones, heightened alertness, and increased heart rate—all aimed at maximizing our chances of survival.

Drawing parallels to financial decision-making, the brain's fight-or-flight response often manifests when individuals perceive threats to their financial well-being. This could include economic downturns, market volatility, or personal financial crises. The brain's ability to recognize and respond to these threats plays a crucial role in shaping financial behaviors.

Financial stress triggers the release of cortisol, the primary stress hormone. This physiological response mirrors the fight-or-flight mechanism, highlighting the intimate connection between our survival instincts and financial decision-making. At the core of the fight-or-flight response lies the amygdala, a small almond-shaped structure in the brain responsible for processing emotions, including fear and pleasure. In financial decision-making, the amygdala plays a pivotal role in assessing risks and rewards, influencing our responses to various financial stimuli.

Risk assessment in investments becomes evident as the amygdala is involved. Perceiving potential financial losses can trigger an amygdala response, leading to heightened emotional reactions that may drive individuals to avoid certain investments perceived as threatening. Research indicates that the amygdala is activated not only by actual financial losses but also by the anticipation of losses. This emotional response contributes to the avoidance of negative financial behaviors as individuals seek to protect themselves from perceived threats.

As humans, our evolved survival instincts deeply influence our behavior, and understanding these connections sheds light on how individuals instinctively avoid root negative financial behaviors. The inclination to avoid financial threats aligns with our evolutionary survival instincts. Just as our ancestors sought to avoid physical dangers, modern individuals instinctively steer clear of financial pitfalls to safeguard their economic well-being. The brain's avoidance mechanism is closely tied to the brain's emotional processing centers. Negative experiences, such as financial losses, can leave a lasting impact on the brain, contributing to a heightened aversion to similar situations in the future.

While the fight-or-flight response and avoidance behaviors are deeply ingrained, understanding cognitive biases can empower individuals to make more informed financial decisions. Loss aversion, a prominent cognitive bias, amplifies the impact of financial losses on decision-making. Individuals are more likely to go to great lengths to avoid losses than to pursue equivalent gains. Recognizing this bias allows individuals to make more rational financial decisions.

Confirmation bias, the tendency to seek information that confirms pre-existing beliefs, can hinder objective financial decision-making. Overcoming this bias involves actively seeking diverse perspectives and considering a range of information before making financial choices. The anchoring effect, where individuals rely heavily on the first piece of information encountered when making decisions, can lead to suboptimal financial choices. Being aware of this bias allows individuals to critically evaluate information and avoid being anchored to irrelevant data.

As we unravel the connections between the brain's fight-or-flight response and financial behaviors, parallel strategies emerge that highlight the adaptive nature of these mechanisms. The brain's fight-or-flight response and financial avoidance behaviors both inherently involve risk mitigation. In the face of perceived threats, individuals naturally seek strategies to minimize risks, whether it be through diversifying investments or creating financial safety nets. The brain's ability to learn from experience and adapt is mirrored in financial decision-making. Individuals who have faced financial challenges often develop a heightened awareness of potential threats, influencing their subsequent behaviors to avoid negative financial outcomes. Both the brain and financial behaviors demonstrate the capacity to build resilience. Through learning and adaptation, individuals can develop strategies to cope with stressors, whether they be physiological or financial in nature.

In navigating the complex landscape of financial decision-making, the brain's fight-or-flight response emerges as an integral player, influencing avoidance behaviors to protect against perceived threats. Understanding the parallel strategies employed by the brain and financial decision-making allows individuals to navigate these realms more consciously, fostering financial well-being while recognizing the evolutionary roots that shape our responses. As we journey through the intricate connections between survival instincts and financial behaviors, a deeper comprehension emerges, offering insights that empower individuals to make informed, adaptive decisions in the face of economic challenges.

4

HIGH JUMP

—◦◦◦—

L ast chapter we closed with putting emphasis on the mental environment that our brain produces when it comes to our financial decision making. Just like anything in life, the ability to make something move starts with your mental ability to believe that it is possible. One may not always know how a thing will come to fruition, but as long as one believes that it can come into fruition is where the real impact starts.

It was rare for me to feel that I couldn't do something, or that a task was too hard and may actually be out of my reach. I never succumbed to that emotion until my eighth grade year on my middle school track team. I was an athlete, but basketball was my jam. I just knew that I was going to become the next Michael Jordan. But hey, eighth grade in middle school, you're the big man on campus, and as a multiple-sport jock, you were the talk of the school.

Although basketball was my first love, and my mom had convinced me that I wasn't a football player because of her fear of me getting hurt, track was the next best thing. I went to tryouts, trash talked with my homeboys on who was the fastest. Tryouts were a formality, we already knew we were on the team, we were the fastest boys in the school!

I was fast, but I wasn't the fastest on the team. I was in the top five of the sprinters. I could have ran the 100 and 200 relays, but my coach was smart and had a keen eye for scoping and developing potential. My coach saw it being most beneficial to let the four fastest sprinters be the sprint team, and he moved me to field events.

"Gaudet," he called. "I'm moving you to jumps."

I said, "Coach, I never did this before, I don't know what to do."

He said, "Don't worry, I'll teach you."

My events were the long jump, high jump, and triple jump. The first couple practices and meets, I hated him, I thought he hated me. I was like why would he put me in something I don't know how to do? I also hated field events because they were always first and none of my friends would get to the meets in time to see me.

My coach trained me for six weeks before we had our first big meet. While I was practicing, I didn't have a reference point of the type of training I was getting because I had not competed against anyone. I was still self conscious about my ability because this was the first time that I did any of these events and I was just following his lead.

I competed in my first meet and I placed first in every event. Not only did I place first, but I found myself criticizing the other athletes. "His form isn't right." "He needs more air in his jump." It became obvious at that moment that they didn't get the same training I was getting.

I remember during practice my coach telling me, "Gaudet, you can jump out of the gym, but with training, you can jump to the moon."

I went on that year to win MVP in the field and broke the eighth grade triple jump record.

Change is uncomfortable, but having a coach, a good coach, is monumental. Having positive money behavior is not inherited, it's taught and if you weren't born into a family of wealth, your family, in most cases, can't teach something that they never experienced. So, by default, you learn what they know, and the cycle continues.

I share the story of me becoming a track athlete for the first time in eighth grade because what he was teaching wasn't about track. Developing a positive relationship with money isn't about success, or how you can buy the dopest foreign. It's the foundational aspect that will affect the rest of your life. Until you know why you do something, you can't take the necessary strides to correct it.

On the court, my off leg was weak, so I couldn't dunk with two hands. My coach saw this, and knew that my triple jump workouts would help to correct this. He knew that I was a basketball athlete and he saw that I had raw talent that needed to be tamed, polished, and nurtured to get me to the next level.

Every one of us is intelligent, but money management isn't a natural instinct. As men and women, we have maternal and paternal instincts, things that we naturally know how to do and may take advanced practice to master, but our finances is not something that any one of us could tackle instinctively.

You have to be real with yourself. I talked about my coach, Coach Allen because I didn't understand what he was trying to teach me. He knew that training me in jumps would make me a better basketball player. He also knew that if I displayed a positive attitude toward something that I wasn't familiar with, and allowed myself to be coached, it would change my life forever. I became MVP by default of being trained on the foundational task to improve myself. I already had the tools, I just needed guidance on how to use them.

When Coach put me in the high jump, the first thing he had to teach me was the arch and thrust. I was only five feet ten inches at the time, so clearing the top height had to deal with more than just being able to jump, the technique had to be on point. You had to be able to jump, bend, thrust, and remain controlled all in one motion. Mastering the technique gave me the ability to defeat athletes that were four to five inches taller than me and might have played the sport longer.

Those that have been able to accumulate mass quantities of wealth have mastered the technique of money management. Some of you have been praying for that slam-dunk day, the day you hit the lottery, or you get the big bonus, and the reality is, you may get it! And then what? Have you ever tried to do something that you weren't trained in, it was awkward, you fumbled a little, you may have even totally messed up whatever you were doing. What do you think will happen with a large cash infusion into your bank account without becoming properly trained? Yep, just like the stories you've heard of people winning the lottery, or getting a big settlement, then three to five years later, they're broke. It's because the money, or the amount of money, was never the issue. It was always their relationship with money and their money behaviors.

Many of you reading this book may have taken the initiative to better your financial situation in some form. Whether you watched a webinar, took a course, went back to school, etc., until you understand the trauma associated with your financial being, changing the way you treat your money will not come into fruition. If you struggle with money and you don't change the way you treat your money, your money won't change the way it treats you.

5

TOP HATS

You heard me mention earlier that my mom was a hustler. Since I was alive, my recollection of her was always business. In 1998, my mom opened our first family business, Top Hats. As a ten-year-old boy, I was extremely proud to have a family business that was displayed at the popular strip mall at the front of our neighborhood. We had the biggest sign on the strip, right at the very top. Everyone in the area knew who my mom was, "The Hat Lady."

It was during that time that I experienced the importance of how the ability to manage cash going in and out is a critical skill. I witnessed first hand the time, commitment, and obstacles that come with starting a business. My mom would drag my baby sister and me to thrift stores for discounted accessory racks, manikins, decorations, and anything else that we needed to stock the shop so that she could save on cost.

My mom had the vision and my grandmother supported it. My grandmother, as a silent investor, invested the seed money for my mom to pursue the venture. My parents were opportunists, and weren't afraid of taking risks. I found through my own business endeavors that taking on risk without mastering the art of money management can become a disaster.

Although our hat shop was not my father's dream, he believed in my mom enough to work a few extra shifts temporarily to assist with some of the start-up cost. He firmly expressed to my mom that he wouldn't have any part of the operations of the business, and its failure or success would solely be based on my mom's ability to bootstrap and turn it profitable.

People say don't mix business with personal, but 99.9 percent of the time, your personal habits translate to your business. My mom was great at what she did. Men from all over the state would travel to our store to allow her to outfit them with the most prestigious "Top Hats" so they could strut their stuff in the New Orleans nightlife. She was talented, she could make anyone look good with the right hat.

But just like our home life, our money script was spending. Our family business wasn't built with a financial strategic plan, or with cash reserves. Our business was born with the same financial mentality that was used in the Gaudet household on a daily basis. Earn, spend, earn, spend, and when nothing is left, rob Peter to pay Paul.

My parents divorced two years after we opened the business. In 2004, I helped my mom close the doors to a business that I was there to see her start. That was a profound moment for me. The look of defeat I remember seeing on her face, no matter how much she tried to hide it. That moment killed the entrepreneur in me. The lesson I took from that experience and from the further perspective of my mom, was that entrepreneurship was too inconsistent, and it wouldn't provide stability.

Your relationship with money will determine how you view the validity of a potential venture. Going into business before fixing your personal financial house is a recipe for failure. You will have a great business idea, and may even have some money to pull it off, but because you have not developed positive financial habits in your personal finances, you will duplicate the same habits in your business. A business is never designed to pay you immediately, and when we start a business with that expectation, we fail financially and emotionally. Our family business did not fail because my mom wasn't a good entrepreneur or the business didn't make money. It failed because she wasn't personally financially stable, therefore, she could not initiate financial preparedness in her business. My mom relied on my father's income for sustainability for necessities while she built the business. She thought she had time and was not prepared for hardship.

I studied my mom growing up. I studied how she talked to people, how she handled business, how she got things done. I learned to do the same thing. I also studied how she used money. I was a natural-born hustler and I could sell you air in a bottle. I knew how to get money, but I could never get money to do what I mentally thought it should do. Deep down, I knew that I should be able to get my money to stretch further than it did, but my relationship with money was too entrenched in consumerism, causing me to use my money in ways that did not promote a solid financial foundation.

I had a saying with my homeboys that I would later grow to hate. "Don't cheat yourself, treat yourself." I would say that often when I wanted to justify spending money in a way that didn't serve me. This went back to my experience in college, having such a negative relationship with money that I developed a money-replacement concept. This meant that if I spent an unexpected amount of money, I would just make the money that I spent to cover the bank account depletion. These times in my life, wealth accumulation was an anomalous hell, I don't even think I knew the word.

This goes back to my earlier point of making a personal money health decision. If you are tired of living life on earth without the means to live life to its fullest, meaning you are tired of having to worry about your use of funds, today you have to decide to become money-trained. See as adults we are only upset about spending money when we don't have it to spend. We only feel that we don't have it if your money isn't in a vehicle where it's earning for you, then you are physically earning every dollar and your stewardship over those dollars determine your outcomes and your family's outcomes. So, you dread when school starts because you know your kids will need new school shoes, or when Christmas comes because you feel you are never prepared and you're tired of getting loans to buy gifts, or taking a vacation and feeling anxiety on the way home because you spent the rent money.

All of these examples are negative money behaviors. I know this because this was me and I'm here to tell you the only way to make it out of the financial whirlwind is to identify where you are and develop a true financial plan. But you can't just have a financial plan, you have to know how you view money and work to adjust that viewpoint. Your plan will give you the roadmap, but knowing and correcting your money beliefs will turn you into a wealth-building machine.

6

THE SHOEBOX

The skill of saving money is more mental than it is ability. People save money for different reasons, but those who desire to accumulate wealth must know that you cannot save your way to wealth. Building wealth is a lifestyle. It's a continuing habit that involves a combination of patience, discipline, values, health, education, sacrifice, and money.

The other financial personality type that one may resonate with is "The Saver". The Saver is an individual that has developed a habit of saving money, but their savings have no objective. This person has undoubtedly experienced some form of past financial trauma because their sole objective for their savings is to have the ability to survey their account balance to overcome financial insecurity. This individual does not have an actual plan for their money and is extremely risk averse. Their aversion to taking risk comes from a fear of not having, these individuals will hoard money in the same fashion as the person that collects old antiques and refuses to give any away. The downfall with this type of relationship with money is this individual believes that they are practicing sound financial habits. While it is a great discipline to develop the consistent nature to put any sum of money to the side, it is a grave disadvantage to not allow your money to work with a purpose.

The time value of money is a financial concept that highlights the idea that a sum of money has different values at different points in time. In essence, it recognizes that the purchasing power of money can change over time due to factors like inflation and the potential for investment returns.

During one of my financial masterminds, I met a lady by the name of Tara Jang. One of the practices that we exercise during our financial workshops is a financial therapy session where we work with attendees on identifying where their money beliefs stem from.

The financial environment that we were raised in is the foundational programing that we will either succumb to or work to get away from. Those that are unsuccessful from getting out of the financial bondage they were raised in, in most cases, have not identified their financial trauma.

Your money belief is directly correlated with how you were raised to perceive money. If you were raised to value money as a tool that created opportunity that was used to help others and to generate more money, chances are you have an abundance mindset and will not approach financial situations with a scarcity-and-lack mentality. If your historic money disposition was centered around survival and consumption, you more than likely approach money with a scarcity mentality.

Tara Jang is a forty-six-year-old woman with two adolescent children and was recently divorced. Jang expressed that over the past thirty years, she has been carrying over $500,000 in savings. When I asked her about her plans for the money, she said she had no plans. She further stated that she and her siblings grew up very poor and they never had money. She said the last thirty years of her life she had made a decision to save the majority of her family's income. They didn't go on trips, celebrate birthdays, or enjoy eating out. Out of fear of not having money, Jang hoarded her money for the latter part of her life. This behavior eventually caused distress in her marriage, causing her husband to file for divorce.

Her perspective of money was to ensure that her family never had to experience deprivation by making sure that money was always present. In this process, she did the very thing to her family that she wanted to avoid, she deprived them. The biggest misconception about budgeting and saving is that you have to deprive yourself. Most of us have the ability to afford more than we give ourselves credit for. The problem that most of us fall into is a true lack of discipline.

For instance, if you want to go to Sunday brunch, you will spend approximately $80 for the outing. But you were going to spend $80 from a necessity item. You will still have the same opportunity two Sundays from now. The difference from you going this Sunday and the Sunday after next, is you want the now factor. Your desires are fighting against you accepting delayed gratification. The key word here is delay. Anything that we do that we plan for, we still get to enjoy it the same, sometimes ten times more when we have mentally, physically, and financially prepared for it. When budgeting, you should always include in your budget money for you to enjoy life. Your human and deprivation is not a healthy form of growth.

Tara Jang's inconsistency with her thought process was that, although she developed the sound habit of saving, she did not make a positive connection with her money, which in turn still made the money unavailable.

Let's dissect her money decision vs if she would have allowed her money to work for her:

Jang's Scenario:

- **She** saved $500,000 over **thirty** years.
- She did not believe in investing and had a negative relationship with money.
- Her savings strategy involved avoiding luxury items, eating out, and any form of investment.

Assumptions:

- We'll assume an average annual inflation rate of 3 percent.
- We'll consider a hypothetical investment with an annual return of 5 percent.

Scenario A: Jang's Savings Without Investing:

She chooses to keep her $500,000 in a savings account without investing.

After thirty years, due to inflation eroding the purchasing power of money, the actual value of her savings would be significantly less than the initial $500,000. Let's calculate this:

Future Value = Present Value × (1–Inflation Rate)
(Number of Years)

Future Value = Present Value × (1–Inflation Rate)

(Number of Years)

Future Value = $500,000 × (1–0.03)30

Future Value = $500,000 × (1–0.03)

30

Future Value ≈ $270,157.50

Future Value ≈ $270,157.50

After thirty years, her $500,000 would have the purchasing power equivalent to approximately $270,157.50 in today's dollars.

Scenario B: Jang's Savings with Investment:

Now, let's explore what could have happened if she had a positive relationship with money and decided to invest her savings.

Using the same future value formula for investments:

Future Value = Present Value × (1+Investment Return)
(Number of Years)

Future Value = Present Value × (1+Investment Return)

(Number of Years)

Future Value = $500,000 × (1+0.05)30

Future Value = $500,000 × (1+0.05)

30

Future Value ≈ $1,449,574.24

Future Value ≈ $1,449,574.24

If she had invested her $500,000 with a 5 percent annual return over thirty years, the future value would be approximately $1,449,574.24.

Comparison:

- Without investing, her savings would have the purchasing power of around $270,157.50.
- With a 5 percent annual return from investing, her savings could have grown to approximately $1,449,574.24.

This comparison illustrates the significant impact of the time value of money and the potential benefits of investing over a long period. It emphasizes the importance of a positive relationship with money and making informed financial decisions to maximize wealth accumulation over time.

Revealing how these early perceptions manifested in extreme hoarding tendencies with her finances, she reflected and disclosed that: "Even though I was proud, it showed me that at this time, having a cash flow was so important. How to have the skillset to manage cash flow."

As Tara Jang approached the concept of saving money, a commendable practice for many, her deeply rooted fear of wealth hindered her from fully embracing its benefits. So, while she was approaching saving money as being commendable, her fear of it limited her growth potential.

To truly prepare for a sound financial future, understanding the time value of money is key. Even when investing, investing in an asset that does not serve you, your family, or your future financial goal is not a beneficial investment. Many without the understanding of this concept will make money decisions with no baseline of why they made it. Tara Jang hoarded a six-figure savings and deprived her family of luxuries and memories and even the ability to grow the savings to create a generational money pipeline because of fear.

In reading this, I want to make sure I stamp this for you: preparation negates fear. It's no way to be fearful of something that you have developmentally prepared for. If you have a big speech, but you have been practicing for weeks, sure you will have some jitters, but you will not be fearful, because you were ready for it. The same applies to your money. Your money has to have a mission and you have to be the general.

7

GOT MILK

February 8, 2003, was a forever turning point in my life. Two days after my fifteenth birthday, I became a father. Every man that is mentally preparing for their child to enter the world has the same thought, how will I support this life that I'm bringing into the world? My parents divorced two years prior, and that situation already left us in a financially constrained environment. I still vividly remember the day my mom bought my sister and me a hamburger to share while she went to sleep hungry.

Having a child at fifteen is an emotional rollercoaster, but increasing the burden of a financially constrained environment is an emotion that is unexplainable. At fifteen, while my peers were thinking about going to the high school jamboree, or the school dance, I was mentally preparing to understand how to earn a living in an environment that was not meant for me to earn a living. The reality is, that's not God's way. A boy can't become a man at fifteen because a man is made through guidance and experience, and at fifteen years old, it's impossible to have mastered either of the two.

During this time was my first experience with my money triggers. Money triggers can manifest in many ways, such as being ignorant about what's going on with your money or feeling panicky anytime money is mentioned. When money comes up, you might suddenly feel more depressed or have a level of anxiety that you didn't feel before. When this happens, stop and think about what money really means to you and what it actually does for you. I was a father now, with no money and no real foresight on how to get any legally. I was embarrassed, ashamed, and disappointed, even more so that we were already broke and my actions made it worse.

This particular day, I was out with my boys. One of my best friends at the time had a car and we were at the local gas station. My son's grandmother was leaving Walmart and she spotted me, she pulled over to the passenger seat window and shouted, "You got some money for milk and diapers?" My answer was no.

Leaving the situation embarrassed, but more importantly confused, I asked myself, why didn't I have money? It wasn't because I didn't want it, it wasn't because I couldn't get any. It was solely because I had not developed my personal relationship with money and even having a child couldn't help me develop that. I didn't have a why! I didn't understand why money was necessary beyond the norm. I knew the norm of what we are taught, which was survival, but survival is in the eye of the beholder. So, if your only money consciousness is from survival, you will never obtain financial freedom because survival has a ceiling. Once you have fulfilled the immediate need, your default setting will say you have done enough, and this will always put you in a state of comfort.

When you are earning to survive, you will require the bare minimum from your money. You need transportation so you will earn enough money for a car, or to make sure the note is paid. That car needs gas but you will only earn enough to fuel your tank to get you to work. You're hungry so you earn enough to eat, you need clothing so you earn enough to purchase your favorite outfits. See, you have very little expectation of your money when in reality your money can work harder than you ever can. The question is, why don't we think this way? Why don't we look at our money as a tool for financial independence? The answer is your programming, your training. We were trained to work, trained to earn, but not trained to manage our finances.

The impoverished community has been taught that money and resources are used to survive. This is far from the truth, money is a tool and should always be used as such. It's a tool to produce and give you the freedom to fulfill your God-given purpose on this earth. At fifteen, how was I going to know this? Who was going to teach me this, my mom? My dad? How could they, they weren't money-trained, my peers weren't money-trained, their parents weren't money-trained, so the dollar that circulated around our community was solely for survival.

It's this money mindset that keeps us in a 360-degree cycle of stagnation. To get off that merry-go-round and be able to hop on the vertical train to wealth, you have to know why you earn and become intentional about your relationship with your money. You must get trained on how to make your money serve you. Remember it's not about the amount, it's about how you use it.

8

SCHOOL SHOES

In the earlier chapter I talked about financial triggers. These triggers can be dangerous if they aren't identified and channeled. Those triggers have a breaking point. We all have read about or heard of people that have committed egregious crimes that involve money, and we sit back and say, "What made them do that?" That is a true example of a financial trigger. A human whose back is against the wall financially is capable of almost anything. Lack, or the fear of losing, without the development of the mental wherewithal is a dangerous recipe when combined with the financial trigger.

The summer going into my sophomore year in high school was tough. I had a new baby, we were struggling financially, and at this point I had very little contact with my father—money was tight. I remember the day my mom came to me and said that my sister and I would have to wear our uniforms and sneakers from the year prior. My sister burst out crying. I understood that my mom just couldn't do it. But it wasn't in her character to be tight, and I could see the pain on her face to even have to tell us that we were so financially constrained we couldn't afford to start the school year off with new clothes and shoes.

That was my breaking point. It was a series of events that led me to engage in behavior that, at the time, seemed to be a means to an end. The inability to properly support my son was my first encounter with my money trigger, and the additional financial burden it placed on my mother was the breaking point. I felt that everyone was suffering because of my decisions, so from my perspective, something had to be done.

I was against selling drugs. My best friend got into the drug game first and I silently hated that he did it. The reality was I envied his ability to earn and spend money so frivolously, but at the time I didn't know that was the emotion I was dealing with. I watched him blow money on clothes, shoes, and gifts for his girlfriend. I would comment, "I would never spend that much money on a pair of shoes." Outwardly lying to myself, I shunned him for it because the reality was, I felt that no matter how much money I made, I had another mouth to feed. So, I could never justifiably do what he did.

At sixteen years old, I got into the drug game. I promised myself that it would be a short-term hustle, only for the summer, enough to make the money needed to buy my sister and me some shoes and uniforms for school, that was the plan.

There was more than one problem with the plan. I didn't have a calculated strategy, my money actions were tied to a negative emotion, and I was earning for survival. Those key factors alone in any situation will lead you into a financial whirlwind.

I accomplished what I set out to do, but I broke the promise to myself. I continued to sell drugs after that period, the reason being is, after I bought the items that we needed, I only had a couple hundred dollars left. I had two options with the capital I had left, walk away with what I had, or re-up and get back to it.

My inability to identify my negative money behaviors led me to continue to sell drugs until I was twenty-two years old. During that time, I risked my freedom, my life, and the lives of others to leave with nothing to show for it. There's a reason they refer to the drug game as the trap. Most people in life don't develop a calculated exit strategy for most of the endeavors they embark on. But the same ideology applies to every human being that earns a dollar in any profession. Without a clear financial plan, we all move through life just earning, until we are put in a position where we can no longer earn due to physical, mental, or health limitations.

Anything in life is attainable with a plan. The problem usually lies with us not willing to patiently wait for the plan to take form. I think about the things of this world, everything built organically has the greatest impact and the longest-lasting effect. When farmers plant crops, it takes time to reap the harvest, but the food is the healthiest in its most organic form. Even if you are looking to grow a following on social media, growing organically takes more time, more sweat equity, but you end up with a more engaged community, which in turn gives you a greater result.

The same applies to our money and wealth. Society will push us to the quick hustle. Why is it that someone can work three jobs and still live paycheck to paycheck. Is it that they just can't make enough money? Or is it that their prior decisions have outlived their earning capacity?

It doesn't matter what the vehicle is for you to earn, without identifying your relationship with money and becoming money trained, the end result is the same, you come up with zero. You will work harder, longer, and less efficiently because, in the end, you don't have a clear picture of what you are earning for or how to flip the script with your money.

The theme of this chapter is about taking financial risks without a plan. Making money with a plan and having a strategy for the money always does a 360. It's the reason why so many people have received large sums of money (e.g., lottery winnings, settlement claims, income tax returns, college refund checks), yet the money lasts for only a brief moment.

It's never about the money, it's the training, and those that have mastered the skill have gone on to build exponential financial legacies. We are very accustomed to the financial gurus that have the ability to teach you to earn, invest, trade, flip, or you name it. But the most tangible skill set is missing from all of those ventures.

Wealth isn't built by investing, or starting a business. Wealth is built by mastering the art of money management, the skill set of employing your money at its highest earning potential. Think about it, the guru teaches you how to flip houses, or how to trade stocks, and let's just say you become successful at it. How much of your trading profits, or the income you made from that fix-and-flip, do you think you will strategically put back into the market to work for you?

The reality is that if you have not been trained, the probability that you would put any of your profits to work is highly unlikely because you were coached to earn, not to manage.

9

FREE THROWS

'Ve always loved the game of basketball. From the age of six years old, I couldn't go anywhere without a ball in my hand.

In my neighborhood, when you were a little league ballplayer, you dreamed of making it to middle school to compete on your middle school sports team. That was the introduction to the big league.

When I got to middle school, I was still fairly short. I was 5 feet 5 inches soaking wet and by the time I made it to my seventh grade year, I only grew one inch. After trying out for the basketball team my seventh grade year, I was cut from the team. It wasn't the norm for seventh graders to make the cut, the team was stocked with mostly eighth graders, who, at the time, all looked like the MonStars from Space Jam.

The following year, I was ready. I knew that I had a shoe-in to not just make the team, but secure the spot for the starting guard. And I was right, not only was I an immediate starter, I showed out so much on the court.

My coach asked, "Where were you last year?"

I laughed and said, "You cut me."

After the first three games, I was leading the team in points and steals until one evening in practice, I went up for a dunk and one of my teammates went up with me to block my shot and as my hand was elevating it struck his knee. I fractured my thumb and I had to sit out for half of the season.

A broken hand wasn't enough for me to sit on the sidelines, I loved the game so much. My right hand, which was my dominant hand, had a cast on it. Against my doctor's orders, and totally against my mom's, I spent four months playing pick-up games with one hand. It was during this time that I perfected a very specific skill that, in most cases, is one of the last areas of focus for a teenage baller.

By default, my off hand became stronger because that was the only hand that I could use. Because I only had one hand, a lot of my shots at the rim would either end with a near miss or a foul sending me to the line. I then realized that if I perfected my one arm free throw, I could ultimately score at will.

In the world of finance, just as in basketball, the allure of quick wins and rapid success often take center stage. The fast-paced hustle of life, the lure of instant gratification, and the allure of flashy investments could be just as distracting as the roaring crowd in a stadium. Yet, the true champions of both realms understood the power of discipline and preparation.

Achieving perfection in free throws and attaining financial independence may seem like disparate pursuits, yet a closer examination reveals intriguing parallels. Both endeavors demand a robust mental approach, where discipline, focus, and resilience form the foundation.

Consider the significance of practice in mastering the free throw. Basketball players commit countless hours to refining their technique, honing muscle memory, and cultivating consistency. Similarly, financial independence requires intentional and continuous effort. Learning about personal finance, investing, and budgeting is akin to the repetitive practice that strengthens a player's free-throw skills. Both endeavors necessitate a commitment to ongoing education and improvement.

In the world of free throws, maintaining focus amid distractions is a critical component. The pressure of the game, the noise of the crowd, and the importance of the shot can all affect a player's concentration. In the financial realm, distractions and external pressures also abound. Economic fluctuations, unexpected expenses, and societal expectations can divert attention from long-term financial goals. Success in both arenas demands the ability to remain focused despite external factors.

Resilience is another shared trait. A missed free throw doesn't define a player's overall performance, just as financial setbacks don't determine one's ultimate success. The ability to bounce back from failures, adjust strategies, and stay committed to the larger goal is crucial in both scenarios. In essence, both free-throw shooters and those striving for financial independence must embrace setbacks as opportunities for growth rather than insurmountable obstacles.

Moreover, the mental strength required for free throws is not only about handling pressure but also making split-second decisions. A player must assess the situation, consider their technique, and adapt to the circumstances—all in a matter of seconds. This quick decision-making mirrors the financial world, where individuals must navigate various options, assess risks, and make informed choices in a dynamic environment.

Analogous to the free-throw shooter visualizing success before taking the shot, individuals on the path to financial independence often benefit from envisioning their goals. Mental imagery and goal-setting are powerful tools that foster motivation and help overcome challenges. Both situations require a clear vision of success to guide actions and decisions.

Furthermore, free-throw shooters and those pursuing financial independence share the experience of dealing with external expectations. In basketball, fans, coaches, and teammates may have expectations for a player's performance. Similarly, societal norms and familial expectations can influence financial choices. Overcoming external pressures and staying true to one's own strategy is a common challenge.

The discipline required to perfect free throws translates seamlessly into financial discipline. Just as a player adheres to a consistent practice routine, individuals seeking financial independence must cultivate discipline habits, such as saving, investing, and avoiding unnecessary debt. Both endeavors necessitate the ability to make sacrifices in the present for future success.

A missed free throw can be a turning point in a game, just as a financial setback can alter the trajectory toward independence. Adversity tests character, and it is during these challenging moments that the mental fortitude of a free-throw shooter aligns with the resilience needed to navigate financial struggles. Embracing challenges as opportunities to learn and grow is essential in both arenas.

Moreover, the element of competition in basketball shares similarities with the competitive nature of the financial world. In sports, players compete against opponents, striving to outperform and achieve victory. Similarly, in the pursuit of financial goals, individuals often face competition, whether it's for job opportunities, investment returns, or reaching milestones ahead of peers. The ability to compete effectively while maintaining integrity is a shared attribute.

In both scenarios, a strategic approach is paramount. Free throw shooters strategically aim for the optimal trajectory and release, adjusting based on the defense's tactics. Likewise, individuals navigating the financial landscape must develop a strategic mindset. This involves crafting a personalized financial plan, adapting to economic changes, and making well-informed decisions to optimize outcomes.

The mental aspect of free throws and financial independence intertwines further when considering the impact of support systems. In basketball, teammates, coaches, and fans contribute to a player's mental resilience. Similarly, individuals on the path to financial independence benefit from a strong support network, whether it's family, mentors, or ultimately a financial advisor. Collaborative efforts and shared goals enhance the journey in both realms.

Furthermore, the concept of "clutch" moments in basketball, where players excel under intense pressure, finds an analogy in financial decision-making during critical junctures. Whether it's negotiating a salary, making significant investments, or navigating economic downturns, individuals must exhibit a "clutch" mentality, making sound choices when the stakes are high.

Creating wealth isn't about luck or happenstance. It's about treating each financial decision with the same level of seriousness as a game-deciding free throw. The outcome of that shot could change the course of the entire season, just as a well-informed investment could shape the trajectory of a person's financial future.

An elite player knows that becoming a master of the free throw requires relentless training, not mere practice. It is about honing one's skills, developing a routine, and refining every aspect of the shot until it becomes second nature. The same holds true for building wealth and becoming financially independent—it demands dedication, education, and a commitment to continuous improvement.

As the days turn into weeks and the weeks into months, a player can delve deeper into the art of the free throw. They can scrutinize their form, study the mechanics, and absorb every bit of wisdom from coaches and mentors. The journey is filled with moments of frustration and doubt, but if the player locks in and is fueled by the unwavering belief, true mastery will be within reach.

In the pursuit of financial independence, you have to approach your goals with the same fervor. You can devour books on investing, seek guidance from financial experts, and carefully craft a well-defined strategy. But if you don't make the mental connection with your finances in understanding how you earn, spend, and invest, when you get the bag, you will fumble.

The lessons learned from the free-throw line served as a constant reminder that success was not bestowed upon the lucky, but earned by those who were willing to put in the work, to train hard rather than merely practice. Just as the ball had to pass through the hoop flawlessly, each financial decision had to be deliberate and well-executed.

It has to be that serious for you, just as serious as "if I miss this shot, the season is over." How many times have you missed your financial shot?

10

EDUCATED FOOL

My senior year in high school was extremely unconventional. Still to this day, I can remember my first week of school. It was everything a young man in his senior year could ask for. I had popularity and freedom. I had completed all my core subjects, so all I had was electives. I had the privilege of getting early release, so I had dismissal at 11:30 a.m., and to top it all off, I had a job interview with the local sheriff's department.

School started off right. Typical in South Louisiana, that week of school we were hit with a hurricane warning. Like usual, we didn't really take it seriously. We were used to hurricane scares and nothing happening. I remember that Friday I went to the football jamboree and the weather was so perfect, breezy, not hot and muggy as usual. Little did we know, after that weekend, life as we knew it would change forever.

I woke up groggy Saturday morning, still sleepy from the long night before.

My mom was screaming at me from the other room. "Jus, get up and go put some gas in the car." She would do stuff like this often to punish me for staying out all night.

I shouted back, "Put gas in the car for what?"

She said, "We are about to evacuate."

I jumped up. "Evacuate, I'm not going anywhere. I got a job interview in the morning." As if that was the most important thing in the world to me. See in my mind, that was my exit. I started selling drugs two years prior to that, but I always felt it had an expiration date. I didn't like it. I was good at it, but did not want to do it long-term because I believed the stereotype, you could only end up in two places, dead or in jail.

I listened to my mom and went to gas the car and the following day we were off to leave the city of New Orleans.

Due to Hurricane Katrina, I spent the first half of my senior year in unfamiliar territory. We spent the first two weeks in Houston, Texas, until we realized that we would not be able to go back home.

My dad was already living in Atlanta, Georgia. My mom, experiencing extreme financial strain, decided to go find a job to get on her feet while we were away.

With the help of my cousin, we got three plane tickets to Atlanta. My sister, best friend, and I boarded a one-way flight. When we got on the plane, the flight attendant brought me a card, it was from my mom and read, "Mamma loves you both, see you soon." Enclosed with it was her last $100.

We were ruffing it, we shared a one-bedroom apartment in the hood in Atlanta, so by the time we got settled in, we felt right at home. We instantly connected with the dope boys and local hustlers in the neighborhood. I lived in Atlanta for six months before returning home to finish high school in my hometown.

I finished my senior year totally unprepared. I didn't know where I was going to college or what I was even going to college for. All I knew was that I had to go and, from how it was presented to me, all I needed to focus on was graduating and the rest would figure itself out.

The omission of money training in the impoverished household gives the family a false reality about higher education. We thought higher education was going to correct everything that negatively impacted our family financially. We go through college thinking that the day we walked across that stage, we would just fall into a land of opportunity that would allow us to make a great living, pay off all our student loan debt, and give us the lives we always desired.

As an adult, moving through my career, I often wondered what my path would have looked like if I would have understood the impact of studying economics, finance, corporate law, or real estate, when I was making my decision to go to college. I had no clue that investment banking was a career. I had never even heard of it. The stock market wasn't talked about in our neighborhood. The few times I saw it on television, it was just rolling numbers on a screen that we quickly went past.

Even the decision on how and what to study in a higher education setting was based on my money trigger. Survival was the only strategy and the path to achieve it was by any means necessary. We didn't have a college fund. I didn't apply for scholarships, so I got into debt to chase the American Dream.

Back to my money trigger. My example was that entrepreneurship was not a way to earn a consistent living. I already had a child so that path was too risky to support a family. The closest example I had to a stable income was an aunt with a good government job. She was the person who helped us when we needed a few extra dollars or clothes here and there. To me, she was the breadwinner. She was the example of money.

A few weeks before graduation, I asked her what did I need to major in to do what she did. After making a few calls, she called me back and said that my major should be Criminal Justice.

In reflecting on my unconventional senior year and the financial challenges I faced, a valuable lesson emerged. The absence of financial education in my impoverished household led me to pursue higher education without a clear understanding of its financial implications. The belief that obtaining a degree would magically resolve financial struggles was a misconception.

As an adult, I realized the impact of neglecting financial education in my earlier decisions. The lack of exposure to concepts like economics, finance, and investment banking limited my understanding of viable career paths. Money management, a crucial skill, was overlooked, and my path to financial stability was uncertain.

Financial education is a powerful tool that can shape one's future. Understanding the significance of studying economics and personal finance can guide career choices and contribute to long-term financial well-being. While entrepreneurship and unconventional paths have their merits, financial literacy remains a foundation for sustainable success. Let this narrative serve as a reminder that mastering the skill of managing money, though often overlooked, is a key to quietly amassing wealth and building a secure future.

I later asked myself, what did that degree prepare me for. The skill of managing money is a skill that is unpopular. It isn't broadcasted, it's not sexy, but the people that master it amass tremendous amounts of wealth and they do it quietly.

11

LA MARGIE

Diseases can be cured, but with viruses, only the symptoms can be treated. A cancer patient with stage four cancer that has gone through numerous radiation treatments and no longer has the cells or strength to fight, the doctors only have the ability to make them comfortable in their last moments.

Going through life without addressing your money triggers is like getting chemotherapy for cancer. Eventually, something will cause you to deteriorate. It's amazing to believe that human beings actually believe that they will automatically change behaviors that are rooted in them without doing any real personal development. We believe that no matter if we spend the latter part of our life in a certain environment, when we become adults, we will miraculously not carry over those behaviors.

I went off to college at eighteen years old with only a hustler's mentality. This meant that everything I did had the same objective. I believed I could negotiate everything. I would negotiate with my professors on why I deserved more time on my assignment, negotiate with my peers to share their homework that they spent hours preparing, and I negotiated with myself that I should never cheat myself, but treat myself. This motto became a justification to spend whatever I earned to give me immediate gratification.

But why? Was I incompetent? No! Was I illiterate? No! I was disconnected to the root cause of my negative money behaviors. You are trying everyday to figure out why you can't get ahead of yesterday. You are trying to figure out why you make a vision board every year but you can't be consistent past April. You are trying to figure out why you can't just save money for vacation instead of borrowing money. It's not because you are incapable of earning, incapable of saving, or incapable of investing. You have not addressed the root cause of your negative money behaviors.

My incapability to identify my money triggers almost cost me my life and potentially the life of someone else. My money script was spending combined with hustling, so my financial makeup had no foundation. My earnings were inconsistent, which always left me behind. I always owed more than I earned and when I hustled to make something come in, it was gone before I got it.

Earning begins to feel obsolete when you never see the money you earn because your earning has no real purpose. Many of us have these money behaviors, but most of us don't know why.

At this time in my life, I couldn't understand why, no matter if I made $100 one day and $1,000 the next day, I would still arrive at the same result: broke by day three. The inability to identify these money triggers put me in a state of constant survival mode. I really couldn't enjoy any of the fruits of life because I was constantly looking for the microwavable harvest.

You don't plant, you don't nurture, you don't prune, and for that reason you don't harvest a crop.

My wake-up moment was the day I decided that I was going to rob the neighborhood dope boy. October 12, 2008, I was a sophomore in college. All of my methods of getting money at the time seemed to have stopped. We were in the middle of a global financial crisis. I just had a newborn baby, there was a drought on the streets, and my connect went to jail.

Mentally, things couldn't have gotten any worse for me. I can remember hanging at some friends' apartment, lying on the floor, staring at the ceiling. I looked over at my best friend, got up, and told him to follow me.

At that moment, my mind was made up. If I was going to do this, we were going to do it big. We grabbed our guns and proceeded to camp out outside the drug dealer's house. We got all the way to his house, jumped the fence, and waited in the dark on the side of his carport. All odds were against us at this point, we had limited ammo and didn't know what to expect if we got into his house. I thought to myself, "What am I doing, this isn't me?" But I was triggered. I was at the point of no return! My friend looked at me and said, "Bro, this ain't gonna work, let's get out of here."

I listened, and we got out of there, but I still wasn't done.

The money trigger unchecked will put you in a drunken state. It will make you do things that could be detrimental to you and your family.

That target was too big for us with such little preparation, so we needed to find an easier target. We circled the neighborhood until we found some guys hanging outside. I drove to the next block, parked the car, and we walked down the street to where they were. And there it was, in a matter of seconds we ran at those guys with guns drawn, demanding they drop to the ground and empty their pockets. After about thirty seconds, we hightailed it back to the next block, hopped in the car, and drove away

The unchecked money trigger can make you unrecognizable to yourself.

Here I was, a college student, criminal justice major, father of two, and leading an armed robbery. Our take from that encounter was a couple of IDs, $200, and an empty wallet. The lesson in this experience is: so many of us have committed ungodly acts that stemmed from a financial hardship that put us into a mental shoebox.

Taking control of your money behaviors is just as important for your mental health as it is for your financial health. It could be the very thing that saves your life.

12

THE HOUSE ROOM

—◦◦◦—

U nderstanding the profound influence of relationships on our financial behaviors often goes overlooked. As mentioned in an earlier chapter detailing my family's money scripts, it became clear that these ingrained behaviors extended into my adulthood and, subsequently, my marriage.

In 2011, I met my wife, and after a year and a half of dating, we married in September 2013. Our financial backgrounds differed significantly. While my parents exhibited a spender's dynamic, my wife's upbringing involved a diligent working father who believed in saving and frugal spending, contrasting with her mother's more lavish and spendthrift approach.

The clash of these money scripts became evident as we navigated our financial journey together. My wife, with a saver's mentality, leaned toward security through saving, yet struggled with wealth accumulation due to a risk-averse nature. On the other hand, my spender habits were drawn to indulgent purchases, illustrious trips, and extravagant items.

Despite my initial reservations about entrepreneurship, my wife, driven by an entrepreneurial spirit, proposed that we venture into business together. At that time, I was set on climbing the corporate ladder and viewed business as an unstable and risky endeavor.

Upon marriage, the combination of our money scripts and triggers became apparent. I was a spender, enticed by luxury, while my wife was a saver, valuing financial security. The challenge arose when one script began to outweigh the other, largely influenced by the absence of identified and addressed money triggers and personalities.

The turning point came in 2014 when my wife suggested moving in with her parents to save money to buy a house. Initially resistant, I viewed this as a step backward. However, this decision, though against my instincts, laid the foundation for our marriage. Living in an eight-by-eight room in her parents' house with a total of ten family members forced us to communicate, be transparent, and build trust—essential elements for a strong foundation.

The initial goal was to save to buy a house, but our plans shifted in the summer of 2014 when my wife was robbed at gunpoint while working at the bank. This traumatic incident led to a period of PTSD, and she decided not to return to work for months. In the midst of this challenge, she reignited her aspiration to start a business.

The first attempt to make the business work was a response to an ad on Craigslist to a small apartment complex. With very little experience in painting and carpentry from helping with small jobs as a kid with my mom, I was definitely out of my league. But I bootstrapped, got my tape measure and clipboard, and went to the walkthrough like I was an award winning contractor.

After completing the walkthrough and submitting the bid, I was anxious to get a response. The property manager called me two days later to inform me that I didn't win the bid. Disappointed, I asked the property manager how much my bid was off from the other company's. She said that my bid was only $700 more than the winning bid. From that point on, we knew that there was money to be made.

After the failed bid, we embraced the setback as motivation to enter the government-contracting space. My wife, a master researcher, acquired multiple small business certifications, becoming a poster child for the SBA and small business development centers. By 2015, we secured our first government contract, marking the inception of our first business venture.

As our business grew rapidly, so did our income. Some may say that growth is great, but rapid growth when you are not versed in the management of money can cripple you. My negative money habits carried directly over to the business.

By April of 2015, we secured our second contract, a six-figure contract that we took a leap of faith and spent our last $1,500 to secure the required insurance to compete for the contract. No experience, no guidance, just grit and twelve months later, my wife retired me from my nine-to-five to join her full-time in the business.

Our negative money behaviors told us that it was okay to quit my job because we had replaced my income through monthly revenue. The reality was, we were another two years away from being able to cancel a stable income and solely rely on the ups and downs of our business income.

By the second year, we were making $60,000 per month. We convinced ourselves that we were achieving notable milestones such as purchasing land, acquiring cars, and expanding operations across the state. However, our financial trajectory took a downturn due to unchecked spending habits, leading to our first financial failure.

In 2018, we faced a stark reality—we despised the business we had built. The financial success we initially enjoyed lacked substance and purpose. Adrift in negative financial habits, we realized we were six-figure paycheck-to-paycheck earners. My wife emotionally distanced herself from the business, and we closed its doors in 2018, living off savings for the next eight months.

The financial downfall forced a reckoning with our personal habits and traumas. Paying our electricity bill with saved coins stored in our Kentwood water jug high-lighted the need for a fundamental shift in our financial direction. The narrative underscores the profound impact of ingrained money beliefs and the consequences of finan-cial illiteracy. It serves as a poignant reminder of the importance of understanding money scripts, fostering a balance between saving and spending, and acquiring the necessary financial skills for sustainable growth.

By 2019, we found ourselves at a crossroads. The closure of our business prompted us to reassess our finan-cial goals and habits. With a newfound determination, we committed to addressing our money scripts, learning from past mistakes, and cultivating a healthier financial mindset.

Our journey took an unexpected turn when we discovered the world of financial education. Engaging with resources, attending workshops, and seeking guidance from financial professionals became integral to our transformation. We realized that financial literacy was the key to unlocking a more secure and prosperous future.

One crucial lesson we learned was the significance of creating a comprehensive financial plan. Understanding our income, expenses, and long-term goals enabled us to make informed decisions. Budgeting became a powerful tool, allowing us to allocate resources efficiently and avoid the pitfalls of impulsive spending.

Moreover, we delved into the realm of investing. Previously unfamiliar with the potential of making money work for us, we embraced the principles of strategic investing. Diversifying our investments and understanding the risk-return relationship became essential components of our financial strategy.

The importance of an emergency fund also became evident. Through the trials of unforeseen circumstances, such as the armed robbery my wife experienced, we recognized the value of having a financial safety net. Establishing an emergency fund provided us with a sense of security and resilience in the face of unexpected challenges.

As our financial literacy deepened, we revisited the goal of homeownership. Armed with a newfound understanding of mortgages, interest rates, and responsible borrowing, we approached the process more strategically.

The dream of owning a home evolved from a distant aspiration to a tangible goal within our grasp.

By 2020, our commitment to financial education began to yield tangible results. We had not only stabilized our financial position but also started building a foundation for long-term wealth creation. With a renewed focus on financial education, we ventured into the realms of strategic planning, investing, and debt management.

Our understanding of strategic planning extended beyond short-term financial goals. We recognized the importance of setting realistic and achievable objectives for various aspects of our lives. This encompassed not only monetary aspirations but also personal and professional growth. Developing a holistic strategic plan allowed us to align our financial decisions with our broader life objectives.

Investing became a pivotal component of our financial journey. Armed with newfound knowledge, we navigated the complexities of the stock market, real estate, and other investment avenues. Diversification became a cornerstone principle, ensuring that our portfolio could weather the fluctuations of different markets.

Embracing a more sophisticated approach to investing, we explored opportunities for passive income. Realizing the potential of generating money without active involvement allowed us to envision a future where our financial assets worked for us. This shift from active income to passive income marked a transformative phase in our wealth-building strategy.

The realm of debt management also came under scrutiny. Armed with financial literacy, we scrutinized our debts, prioritized repayment strategies, and explored ways to leverage debt for strategic purposes. This nuanced approach to debt transformed it from a burden into a tool that, when used wisely, could contribute to our financial growth.

In parallel, our commitment to education expanded beyond our personal development. Recognizing the systemic issues surrounding financial education in under-served communities, we embarked on a mission to bridge the gap. We started engaging with local schools, community centers, and organizations to provide financial literacy workshops.

The workshops covered fundamental concepts such as budgeting, saving, investing, and debt management. Our goal was to empower individuals with the knowledge and skills needed to navigate the intricacies of personal finance. Witnessing the positive impact on the community reinforced our belief in the transformative power of financial education.

As our financial journey progressed, the importance of mindset became increasingly evident. We delved into the psychology of money, examining the deep-seated beliefs and attitudes that shape financial behaviors. This introspective journey allowed us to identify and challenge limiting money scripts that had hindered our progress.

One key revelation was the impact of generational money scripts. Reflecting on our respective family backgrounds, we recognized the inherited beliefs that influenced our financial decisions. Breaking free from these ingrained patterns required conscious effort and a commitment to redefine our relationship with money.

Our mindset shift extended to the concept of abundance. Embracing an abundance mindset involved cultivating gratitude for the resources at hand and fostering a belief that opportunities for growth were limitless. This shift from scarcity to abundance not only transformed our approach to wealth but also influenced our decision-making and overall well-being.

By 2021, our financial landscape had undergone a remarkable transformation. We had transitioned from a position of financial instability to one of strategic wealth creation. The lessons learned, both through successes and setbacks, had fortified our resilience and equipped us with the tools to navigate the unpredictable terrain of personal finance.

Our commitment to financial education remained unwavering. In addition to community workshops, we explored digital platforms to disseminate information and create an online community focused on financial literacy. The goal was to reach a broader audience and empower individuals beyond geographical constraints.

Reflecting on our journey, we realized that the ability to harness increased income for long-term growth required more than just financial literacy. It demanded a holistic approach that encompassed strategic planning, investing, debt management, and a transformative mindset. The lessons learned through our experiences became the foundation for a comprehensive framework that could guide others on their path to financial prosperity.

As we entered 2022, our financial journey continued to evolve. The experiences of the past decade had instilled in us a deep appreciation for the dynamic nature of personal finance. We embraced the ongoing process of learning, adapting, and refining our financial strategies to align with changing circumstances and goals.

The narrative of our financial journey serves as a testament to the transformative power of education, resilience, and a proactive approach to personal finance. It underscores the notion that financial success is not a destination but an ongoing journey that requires continuous learning and adaptation.

In conclusion, our story offers valuable insights into the multifaceted nature of financial growth. From humble beginnings and financial struggles to strategic wealth creation, the journey encapsulates the importance of knowledge, mindset, and proactive decision-making. As we continue to navigate the ever-evolving landscape of personal finance, our commitment to sharing these lessons remains steadfast, driven by the belief that everyone deserves the opportunity to achieve financial prosperity through education and empowerment.

13

REVELATION HORSE

They say money really highlights the person that you truly are. If you are a giving person, with money you will be more giving. If you are a greedy person, with money, you will be more greedy. But what does an untrained person become when their life instantly changes due to a large cash infusion? You may have sincerely thought about a day or a circumstance that would drastically change your financial situation: winning the lottery or receiving a large inheritance. We often think about how getting more money will benefit us positively, but rarely think about how money can harm us if received before we are prepared.

January 8, 2019, my best friend was killed. He was killed in a motorcycle accident, but I say he was killed by the money. Torian Anderson, we called him "Horse", instantly became rich due to an inheritance from his father passing the year prior.

The funny thing about money is that it is a dictator and if you have not developed the necessary character traits and disciplined habits to dictate it, you lose control. With years of experiencing struggle, this immediate cash infusion in Horse's life fueled a path of living life from the lens of past deprivation. The ability to provide yourself with all the things that you desired when you could not fulfill those desires is a powerful emotion. His newfound wealth gave him the ability to live the life that he desired deep down: drinking, partying, fast cars, motorcycles, he had no limitations, during these moments he felt limitless.

I moved away from our old neighborhood in 2006. Horse remained in our neighborhood in the house he grew up in, once his parents separated, he retained ownership. Life became very different for him over those years. While I went away to pursue my education, he and I remained connected as some of our old money habits were still intertwined. The years in which I attended college that I kept hustling, he was one of my earners back at home. During that time on multiple occasions during the re-up, we would talk about a day of financial freedom.

As I continued to grow and educate myself on how we as black and brown men navigated in this world financially, Horse was my very first ear to listen to the teachings that I would bring back to the hood.

We were connected since I was six. Horse was four years older than me, so he was more like a big brother. He protected me, taught me how to fight, taught me how to stand up for myself in the streets and how to always stand on business. He showed me how to value principles and take diplomatic approaches to situations. The difference between the two of us: he stayed, I left.

The ability to become financially conscious is just as much of an environmental result as it is intellect. Many people become educated and informed but their consistent habitual influence stifles their ability to apply any new teachings that they may have obtained.

Torian and I grew up in the same neighborhood, two houses down from each other. Growing up, he was the kid that had the nice clothes, nice car, etc. I thought they were rich. Of course, myself growing up with a totally opposite environment, no free-flowing money or financially secure father figure, I took my parents divorce as the statement for me to get on the grind. Horse's experience from his parents was the opposite.

When Torian's father passed, at that time in our lives, we were both grown with families. I was thirty years old and he was thirty-four. His father passed leaving him a six-figure inheritance, no will, no guidance, and no instruction. He was the only heir. Although he had a step-brother, he was his father's only biological son.

Statistics say that by 2050, the black wealth in America will be zero. Over the years, we have heard from the financial gurus through ads and social media projects how they will help to change the dynamic of generational wealth in the black community by teaching you how to earn through courses, digital guides, coaching, and master-minds. Generational wealth accumulation has become a popular subject in the black community, but the reality is that the passing down of wealth in the black community has very little to do with money.

The passing down of values is the most lucrative aspect of wealth accumulation. Familial values are the core substance on how wealth can be accumulated, distributed, and passed down. There are many aspects that plague the black community that inhibit the development of core familial values.

It's a harsh reality that you can spend a significant part of your life building a business, investing in real estate, stocks, etc. and due to a lack of values and principles being directly distributed to those survived by you, your wealth won't make it past the second generation. Wealth is a values system built on consistency, teachings, morality, and patience.

One can amass wealth with the right values system, but wealth with the absence of values would be diminished. Due to a lack of familial values, black American families lack the necessary infrastructure needed to successfully sustain generational wealth. This infrastructure comes in the forms of wills, trust, proper insurance, family planning, financial advisory, morality, values, and instruction.

14

TREAT YOURSELF,
DON'T CHEAT YOURSELF

—∞—

Once you identify how you truly value money, it becomes a mirror to your life. Don't get discouraged when you are just beginning your path to developing positive money behaviors and have moments of weakness or inconsistency. Your financial journey is no different than a runner training for a marathon or a fighter training for a boxing match. Ideally, one would work to identify and practice these habits early, but it starts with you, and you hold the responsibility to distribute financial values to the generations behind you.

Your money personality will become the foundation of your financial future. You will notice things about yourself now and compare them to things in the past that you have been practicing for years. But it will make sense because certain things might have felt instinctual and you'll see you were making the excuse of "that's just how I am."

As I've mentioned before, I had extreme negative money behaviors. I was multiple money personalities wrapped in one. Although you will have a dominant personality type, many will resonate with the characteristic traits with multiple types.

There was a point in my life where there was no true authoritative figure in my life. No one that actually held the "shut up" card, as my Apostle Mike Wicker would say. That person whose life you could look at and say,

"Whatever they tell me to do, I'm going to do, because they have the blueprint."

My mom always had my utmost respect, but women raising young men that possess a combination of ambition, intellect, and an adventurous spirit, tend to have a difficult time leading the young men in the direction they desire them to go if there is no alignment of the teachings with tangible assets. By my teenage years, my mom gave me a lot of freedom to make my own decisions, many decisions I look back on now and wish I would have had a more authoritative figure to say, "Boy, sit your ass down."

My natural money disposition was a spender. That was how I grew up, robbing Peter to pay Paul, not really understanding how money works, the importance of savings, and the security of investments. My ambitious nature gave me the eye of the tiger, so I was prone to go out into the world and make things happen. But so many years of tirelessly making it happen without intentional strategy is exhausting.

So what happens in this scenario? What happens when an individual has the characteristics of the Overextender, the Spender, the Investor, and the Avoider? Within this combination of money character traits, this individual has very little respect for money. They see money as a tool to get more and create opportunity, but their lack of positive financial habits puts them at risk to squander any profits made from investments.

This person is not an avoider of money, they actually believe that money can be made in any form, however, they avoid those negative traits about themselves that highlight their negative money behaviors. This person is never short of ideas and they have extreme earning capabilities. They believe that one day, one of the many business deals will put them on a vertical path to wealth creation or the next play is going to be the best play.

The years I spent dealing drugs, I had very little debt. At some points, I had no debt, and for a person generating cash daily but not retaining any to allocate for longevity purposes has to identify the underlying money characteristics that are causing stagnation.

My money journey was a true rollercoaster. By twenty-one, I made my first real estate investment. By twenty-eight, I had a six-figure business. By thirty, I was invested in multiple assets. And by thirty-two, I was what they would call asset rich and cash poor. I found myself overleveraged with extreme financial anxiety.

The toughest part about this period is you have money tied into things that you have convinced yourself are going to make you money. The kicker is, it is going to make you money, but the problem lies within the fact that you made the wrong type of investments for the state that you are currently in.

I wasn't in position to assess this because I had no true money relationship.

In 2016, when our business conducted over twenty house flips, instead of splurging on trips, clothes, and expensive cars, I should have been investing the cash into high-yield investment accounts that would generate cash.

When you are investing, you have to develop an investment criteria. For more seasoned investors, this would be an investment policy statement. This is a roadmap to tell you what you are investing for and the type of investments you should participate in as it aligns to your goals. This becomes your rule book.

At this time in my life, I didn't have an investment criteria, so I had no roadmap for my investments. Due to the fact that I was operating a six-figure business with multiple employees across multiple cities, my investment criteria for that time period should have been to invest to generate cash. The cash that would have been generated could have later been invested into long-term holdings. So, because I didn't invest for cash, I blew the cash. Guess what next phase investing rested on? Yep, you guessed it, credit! Rule of thumb, just because you have good credit, does not mean you're an expert on knowing how to leverage it.

Credit, or OPM (other people's money) as society likes to call it, is a leveraging tool. In the dynamic landscape of finance, credit emerges as a pivotal leveraging tool, empowering individuals and businesses to extend their financial reach beyond immediate means. Credit can open the door to opportunities that would be unattainable with limited cash reserves, which can allow you to access additional funds for various purposes. Seasoned investors strategically leverage credit to finance ventures and real estate, maximizing their potential returns and participating in opportunities that align with their financial goals.

The mistake that I made was leveraging credit without having the cash reserves to support the money I was borrowing. The wealthy will tell you, never use your own money, and this is true. You should always seek to use cheap capital for ventures such as real estate and/or acquiring other businesses, while putting your cash into another vehicle that will work on overdrive. But where many people get caught up, very similar to myself, is leveraging credit for investment purposes without having the liquid capital for a safe haven. This is crucial in the case that your investments don't produce as anticipated, you have enough bandwidth to keep the machine going until it corrects itself.

For businesses, credit becomes instrumental in maintaining and expanding operations, from acquiring inventory to investing in essential equipment, driving growth and competitiveness. Credit's flexibility allows individuals and businesses to act swiftly, capitalizing on time-sensitive investment opportunities without waiting for extensive savings accumulation.

Leveraging with credit aids in risk management, enabling investors to diversify portfolios and spread resources across different assets, potentially mitigating the impact of losses. Responsible credit usage not only provides immediate benefits but also contributes to enhanced creditworthiness, paving the way for better terms on future loans and increased financial leverage.

On a broader scale, the availability of credit in the economy fosters economic growth by supporting business expansion, job creation, and innovation. However, as with any financial tool, leveraging with credit demands prudent management.

Understanding and mitigating associated risks are crucial to harness the full potential of credit as an leveraging instrument. You should not use credit unless you have at least three times as much of your credit limit in cash reserves. This is a core financial habit all the way to the simplest of situations. If you have a credit card with a $300 limit and you want to use this card for groceries and odds-and-ends items, perfect, but you should not use the card to its max unless you have a minimum of $900 in cash reserves that are unallocated for anything else.

Life is extremely unpredictable and when you are working to develop sound financial habits, you may have the best intentions, but when life punches you in the face and you are financially unprepared, you will go into financial regression. This example of the credit card happens to the best of people with the best intentions to build sound financial habits. You received some financial education and you promised yourself, you would no longer use your credit cards to consume, no more frivolous shopping and random brunch outings. You are committed to using the card to build sound financial habits.

Well you do this, you buy groceries and gas and max out the card with the intention to pay the card off on your Friday payday. Then, on Thursday, you get a flat tire, and because you need your car to get to work, you have to make a decision, pay your card off like you promised yourself, or take some of the money and get a new tire. More than likely, while still working through your financial development habits, you will choose the latter. Developing the practice of having three dollars for every one dollar you spend on your credit card will ensure you never fall into consumer debt.

15

TWENTY

$\begin{smallmatrix} \blacktriangleright\!\!\!\!-\!\!\!\!0\!\!/\!\!0\!\!\!\!-\!\!\!\!\blacktriangleleft \end{smallmatrix}$

Becoming financially independent is so much more than just money in a bank account, or the ability to amass any financial desire. In this chapter, I'm going to take this time and use this as my diary.

Jamael Jai'Ron Gaudet, my son, my firstborn, the first reference point of my relationship with my money trigger. I didn't know that, while writing this book, I would tragically lose my son to gun violence. He was twenty years old. I asked myself, if this would be relevant to tell you, what could you get from me sharing this? The only thing I could think of was wisdom! The urge to help someone else avoid feeling the feelings that I have in this moment is jet fuel to influencing my understanding even more of why financial freedom is a requirement, not a goal.

I missed the opportunity to practice this with my own son. One of the hardest things about losing someone, especially a child, is to see the trajectory unfold over time. As a young father, I always knew what I wanted for my son and growing up together, while simultaneously learning the value systems to teach him, you quickly realize that time doesn't wait for you to get it right, but you pray that it will slow down a little to allow you the ability to catch up.

Society has diminished the importance of values. We live in a world where there are extreme barriers in place when attempting to instill positive values into our children and the reality is we can't change the wealth dynamic without addressing this issue. So how can we pass down wealth to our heirs when the probability that the lessons taught at home will be dismantled by external forces? These forces come in many forms: social media, peers, parents, siblings, courts, just to name a few.

According to the US Census Bureau, sixteen percent of children live in blended families, 1,300 new stepfamilies are formed each day, and 40 percent of families in the US are blended with at least one partner having a child from a previous relationship before marriage.

New societal family dynamics have a direct reflection on how wealth is created and distributed, especially in Black American families. In most instances, modern day society has dismantled the unity of the black family.

With almost half of the nation's family dynamic being blended families, we have to take into account, how does one instill morals and values into their heirs when they are more than likely being raised in two different environments, with two different perspectives, and two different influences.

Divorces, custody battles, and child-support disputes are all gory experiences. No party walks away from these situations whole and the children are never sheltered from the emotion that these situations inflict on them.

Reverting back to the development of generational wealth in modern day society, how do we accomplish this? Blended families are not supported by court systems, and societal influence has created a wedge on how blended families should raise a child. I wholeheartedly believe that, if my child is being raised with his mother and significant other, then he has the same right to be a part of the decision-making process when it comes to his well-being. But when do the external resources acknowledge our new normal?

There can be a biological mother and father that are both remarried and the court will exclude the stepparents from the decision-making process of the child. So, the question resides, if a stepparent is raising a stepchild for years, and the stepparent is summoned to court and denied the right to participate in the proceedings, what is the real message distributed to families on how to handle family affairs?

If a child is learning financial responsibility in one home, but then goes to the other home and the narrative on money is "spend everything you earn," there is a direct mental conflict in that child's ability to make a decision on what information is for his or her benefit.

I encourage blended families today to put aside unfinished feelings and raise children as a village. In our financial wellness programs, we counsel blended families on developing financial plans as a blended family, showing both domiciliary and non-domiciliary parents how to boycott the child support enforcement system and put investments in place that will serve as support for the child.

One may say, why would I boycott the child support enforcement system? Let's take a deep dive into the infrastructural makeup of this system. When one parent goes to seek enforcement, they are making a case from some form of negative experience. This experience can be from the factual basis that the non-domiciliary parent is not assisting in supporting the child or current conditions of support are not agreeable to either party.

Either way, historically, it has not been the practice of the state to diplomatically heed the best interest of the family, which has a direct effect on the child. The parameters of child support enforcement totally negates any wealth-building strategy. Think about it, how many wealthy people have you seen sitting in the lobby in a child-support court. You haven't, they handle their disputes with paid mediators and arbitrators. The system is designed to keep one party dependent on the system and another in financial bondage causing strife and negativity between the parents, which waterfalls down on the child.

Our practices not only provide a wraparound financial blanket for the child and family, but a direct step in building a value- and asset-based system that will direct a path to generational wealth. For more information, download the child support freedom guide (www.jaygaudet.com).

At this point in my career, I've been successful. I'm still not to the point where they would say in some of my favorite mafia movies that I'm "a Made Man." Speaking politically correct, I am still on the journey to financial independence.

As an entrepreneur, where your life is funded by what you create, what you produce, even if you have a hundred people working for you, if you have to think about making money, you are not free. This was the most profound loss in my entire life, but I learned quickly that no matter what emotion I'm facing, without achieving financial independence, the necessity to earn doesn't end.

I received the call at 2:56 a.m. on May 10, 2023, that my son was killed in my old neighborhood, three blocks from where we grew up. I mentioned briefly in the chapter "Got Milk," about me becoming a father at fifteen, the turning point of my life.

My parents divorced two years prior and as a result, my younger sister and I spent most days and nights home alone. My mom did the best she could with what she had, but as Jay Z said, nobody wins when the family feuds. I can think back at that time, thinking the only thing that would fix all of the issues that we were facing was money. My parents always argued about money, whether my dad was misusing it or my mom not making enough of it.

Becoming money-trained is not just about becoming rich, or wealthy. Becoming money-trained even has its impact on how and when you start a family. A friend of mine once told me that he wanted to focus on becoming financially free so that when he got married and had children, he could solely focus on his family. Still to this day, those words ring bells in my head because that was the perfect painting of what financial freedom is. In so many cases, people are seeking financial freedom without knowing why.

I challenge you to take a different stance with your money. Can your money outlive you? Are you prepared for financial hardship, prepared to pay for a funeral, able to help a family member with their medication? If your money is just for survival, it will never grow past your own necessity, meaning that you can't obtain financial freedom.

Don't get it twisted, folks. Some of you will go on to earn millions of dollars, but that doesn't mean that you will be financially free. If your relationship with money has not changed in the midst of earning, you will default to the sole characteristic that you have displayed all your life with money. You will just be a six-figure-check-to-check earner.

Being free allows you to do two things. The most important thing any human can contribute during their dash in this world is to live in their purpose. This means that the sole reason that God created you and the greatness He put inside you is you are able to give to the world freely and give Him all the glory. Secondly, your passion, the thing you can do everyday, all day, and you never have to make a dollar doing it. This is what you do when you are financially free, when money is the tool and you are the trained skillsman.

16

THE FOURTH GENERATION

U nderstanding the proximity to legacy hits home when, at thirty-five with teenage children, the realization dawns that, by eighty-five, four generations of heirs might follow. This prompts a profound evaluation of how one navigates the dash—the time from birth to passing—questioning the stewardship of God's bestowed resources.

Legacy, often misconstrued as solely passing wealth to offspring, transcends a mere financial inheritance. True money wisdom asserts that wealth's true purpose lies in making a lasting impact. Alarming statistics reveal that an estimated 70 percent of wealthy families lose their fortune by the second generation, escalating to 90 percent by the third. The crux lies in the inadequate passing down of financial wisdom. The next generation, unacquainted with the journey to prosperity, lacks the grounding principles and values needed to sustain and grow the family wealth. Untrained, they default to consumption, jeopardizing the family's financial legacy.

To counter this trend, instilling money principles and values becomes paramount. Training recipients on the essence of maintaining and growing wealth imparts a perspective that transcends mere consumption. Even if they didn't partake in the initial wealth accumulation, this training fosters respect for the discipline required to leverage money for its highest and best use.

A crucial takeaway emerges: leaving wealth without explicit instructions for its perpetual operation risks eroding the very foundation of one's legacy. The key lies in understanding that wealth, like any other asset, needs a strategic plan for its longevity.

The question then becomes, how does one achieve this? The answer lies in deliberate decision-making. Financial planning must assume a place of prominence in one's life, akin to annual health check-ups, pursuing higher education, or engaging in one's profession. It's a mental priority, a conscious effort to ensure the future resilience and perpetuity of the wealth being amassed.

Beyond the financial realm, a holistic approach involves imparting not just monetary wisdom but also the values and principles that guided the accumulation of wealth. This becomes a narrative, a story of discipline, hard work, and strategic decision-making. The goal is to create a framework that outlasts the initial wealth generator, ensuring that subsequent generations are equipped to navigate the financial landscape responsibly.

Integrating financial education into family culture establishes a foundation for informed decision-making. It transcends the idea of inheritance as a one-time transaction, transforming it into a continuum of shared knowledge, values, and responsibilities. A family's financial legacy then becomes a living entity, evolving with each generation.

Furthermore, legal structures such as trusts and foundations can formalize this continuum. These entities provide a structured framework for wealth management, ensuring that the intended purpose of the wealth aligns with the family's values and goals. Periodic reviews and updates to these structures become essential, reflecting changing family dynamics, economic landscapes, and societal shifts.

In the pursuit of a lasting legacy, communication emerges as a linchpin. Open dialogues about wealth, values, and responsibilities foster understanding and unity among family members. An ongoing conversation ensures that the family's financial blueprint adapts to evolving circumstances, creating a resilient legacy that withstands the tests of time.

Ultimately, the path to legacy involves intentional, ongoing efforts—decisions made today that resonate through generations. It's a commitment to not only accumulate wealth but to nurture it with wisdom, values, and a forward-looking perspective. In this way, the dash between birth and passing transforms into a meaningful continuum, where each generation contributes to a legacy that stands as a testament to resilience, wisdom, and enduring prosperity.

Financial planning must extend beyond personal decisions. It needs to become a shared family endeavor. Engaging the family in discussions about financial goals, values, and responsibilities fosters a sense of ownership. This collaborative approach ensures that each family member understands their role in preserving and growing the family wealth.

One effective strategy is to establish family meetings dedicated to financial matters. These gatherings create a space for open dialogue, allowing family members to express their views, ask questions, and contribute to decision-making. It's an opportunity to educate the younger generation about the complexities of wealth management and the principles that guide it.

Moreover, these meetings can serve as a platform to discuss the family's broader goals, such as philanthropy or social impact initiatives. Aligning wealth with a purpose beyond individual interests reinforces the idea that wealth is a tool for positive change. Integrating charitable giving into the family's financial plan not only benefits society but also instills a sense of responsibility and gratitude in heirs.

In addition to fostering open communication, it's crucial to document the family's financial plan. This formalization process involves creating a comprehensive document outlining the family's values, goals, and strategies for wealth preservation and growth. Legal professionals can assist in drafting wills, trusts, and other legal instruments that articulate these plans and ensure their execution.

As the custodian of the family's financial legacy, an investment manager like myself plays a pivotal role. Beyond financial acumen, I strive to impart the values and principles that underpin wise investment decisions. It's about instilling a mindset that values long-term sustainability over short-term gains, and responsible stewardship over reckless consumption.

To fortify the continuity of the financial legacy, consider establishing an educational fund for younger family members. This fund can support their pursuit of higher education and financial literacy, equipping them with the tools to navigate the complex world of finance. Empowering the next generation with knowledge ensures they are well-prepared to handle the responsibilities that come with wealth.

Continual reassessment of the family's financial strategy is vital. Economic landscapes evolve, tax laws change, and family dynamics shift. Regular reviews of the financial plan and its legal structures allow for necessary adjustments. This adaptive approach ensures that the family's wealth remains aligned with its overarching values and goals.

In essence, the journey to legacy is an ongoing process of refinement and adaptation. It involves a commitment to lifelong learning, resilience in the face of challenges, and an unwavering dedication to the principles that define the family's financial identity. Through deliberate planning, open communication, and a shared commitment to stewardship, the legacy that transcends generations becomes a reality—one where each member contributes to a narrative of enduring prosperity and impact.

To further solidify the legacy, consider establishing a family constitution or mission statement. This document encapsulates the family's core values, guiding principles, and the shared vision for the future. It serves as a compass, providing direction for family members in times of decision-making. A well-crafted constitution becomes a source of unity, ensuring that even as the family grows, there remains a cohesive understanding of what the wealth stands for and how it should be managed.

Embracing technology is another facet of modern legacy planning. Utilize digital tools to centralize and organize important financial information. This not only streamlines the management of assets but also ensures that subsequent generations have easy access to critical details. Moreover, technology facilitates the tracking of investment performance and helps adapt the financial plan to changing market conditions.

While monetary wealth is a significant aspect, it's crucial not to overlook the non-financial components of legacy. Intangible assets such as family traditions, values, and stories are equally vital. Sharing anecdotes of the challenges faced and victories achieved fosters a sense of connection to the family's history. Intergenerational storytelling becomes a means of passing down not only the financial wisdom but also the cultural and emotional aspects that define the family legacy.

Mentorship within the family is a powerful tool. Establish mentor-mentee relationships where younger family members can learn from the experiences and insights of their elders. This not only imparts practical knowledge but also strengthens family bonds. The mentorship model promotes a culture of collaboration, where each member contributes to the collective growth and preservation of the family's legacy.

In addition to intra-family mentorship, seeking external expertise remains valuable. Engage professional advisors, such as financial planners, estate attorneys, and tax experts, to provide objective insights. Their guidance can be instrumental in navigating complex financial landscapes and ensuring that the family's wealth management strategies align with legal requirements and best practices.

Lastly, philanthropy emerges as a powerful means of perpetuating a positive legacy. Establishing a family foundation or contributing to charitable causes reflects a commitment to making a lasting impact on society. Involving family members in philanthropic activities instills a sense of social responsibility and empathy, aligning the family's legacy with a broader, altruistic purpose.

In conclusion, the path to a resilient and enduring legacy involves a multifaceted approach. It encompasses financial planning, open communication, legal structuring, education, technology integration, and a commitment to non-financial aspects like values and stories. This holistic strategy ensures that the family legacy not only survives but thrives across generations, leaving a positive imprint on both family members and the world at large. The journey to legacy is not a destination but an ongoing process—one that evolves, adapts, and continues to resonate through the annals of time.